The Lathe Book

A Complete Guide to the Machine and Its Accessories

Completely Revised and Updated

Ernie Conover

The Taunton Press

Publisher: JIM CHILDS
Editor: HELEN ALBERT
Associate Editor: JENNIFER RENJILIAN
Copy Editor: DIANE SINITSKY
Indexer: LYNDA STANNARD
Cover Designer: LYNNE PHILLIPS
Interior Designer: MARY MCKEON
Layout Artist: ROSALIE VACCARO
Front Cover Photographer: SCOTT PHILLIPS
Back Cover Photographer (author photo): RANDY O'ROURKE
Interior Photographer: ERNIE CONOVER, except where noted
Illustrator: MARIO FERRO

The Taunton Press
Inspiration for hands-on living®

Printed in the United States of America
10 9 8 7 6 5

The Taunton Press, Inc., 63 South Main Street, PO Box 5506,
Newtown, CT 06470-5506
e-mail: tp@taunton.com

Library of Congress Cataloging-in-Publication Data
Conover, Ernie.
    The lathe book : a complete guide to the machine and its accessories /
Ernie Conover.—Completely rev. and updated.
        p. cm.
    Includes index.
    ISBN-13: 978-1-56158-416-1
    ISBN-10: 1-56158-416-9
    1. Lathes. 2. Turning. I. Title.
    TT201 .C66 2001
    684'.083—dc21   00-066300

To my mother and father. Both talented artists, they have always nurtured a quest for knowledge and love of art, craft, and history.

Acknowledgments

Writing a book is a big undertaking, and I would like to thank the following people who were extremely generous with their time and were long-suffering in reviewing material and discussing their opinions: Clead Christiansen; Tim Clay of Oneway Manufacturing; Barrey Frey of Safetronics Inc.; Peter Gill of Robert Sorby Ltd.; Jerry Glaser of Glaser Engineering Company; Dave Hout; Kevin Kee of Delta International Machinery Corp.; Brian Latimer of Teknatool International Ltd.; Darrel Nish of Craft Supplies USA; and Brad Packard of Packard Woodworks. I'd particularly like to thank Teknatool International Ltd. and Woodcraft Supply Corp. for supplying the Nova 3000 on which many of the photos in this book were shot.

I would like to give special mention to my good friends at KSK Color Labs. They ran test clips, pushed, pulled, and normally processed all of the film for this book in an expeditious manner.

I'd also like to thank all of the folks at The Taunton Press, with special mention to Helen Albert and my editor Jennifer Renjilian.

ABOUT YOUR SAFETY

Working with wood is inherently dangerous. Using hand or power tools improperly or ignoring safety practices can lead to permanent injury or even death. Don't try to perform operations you learn about here (or elsewhere) unless you're certain they are safe for you. If something about an operation doesn't feel right, don't do it. Look for another way. We want you to enjoy the craft, so please keep safety foremost in your mind whenever you're in the shop.

Contents

Introduction

In this book, I will share with you my love of the woodturning lathe. This is a book with a difference because it doesn't focus on the lathe to the exclusion of all other woodworking. Rather, it treats the lathe as another essential tool in the woodworking shop—a tool that can expand your woodworking horizon and add pizzazz to your work. All woodworkers need to be more familiar with the lathe because at some point your woodworking projects will require turned parts.

When The Taunton Press asked me to do the second edition of *The Lathe Book*, I was delighted, but I never realized that rewriting is much more difficult than writing. Much has changed since the first edition, so there are many new machines, accessories, and gadgets to share. Turning is becoming gentrified, and there are now tools and accessories that had never before been dreamed of. While the philosophical side of me laments the simplicity lost, the tool junkie side of me opens each "absolutely indispensable" new piece of hardware with childlike enthusiasm. My wife, Susan, appropriately bought me a T-shirt claiming, "He who dies with the most tools wins." I am in serious contention for the grand prize.

I am also a better turner today than I was eight years ago and have taught scores of people to turn, so I can tell the story better. Because I have also written *Turning for Furniture Makers* (a detailed spindle-turning book with an accompanying video) and *Turn a Bowl with Ernie Conover* (an action manual for bowl turners) since the first edition of *The Lathe Book*, I decided to drop some of the techniques and concentrate more on the lathe and it accessories. The tool chapter is much more readable and the illustrations are better. Photography is entirely new and in color.

Turning books generally speak to dedicated turners who pursue turning to the exclusion of all other forms of woodworking. But most woodworkers are interested in turning only enough to use the lathe in their general woodworking. Additionally, most turning books miss the mark because they never really teach you to turn. They talk about equipment, philosophy, and history, but they never truly teach turning. With that in mind, I've tried to keep this a woodturning book that speaks to all woodworkers and gives the information necessary to be able to employ turning in furniture making. This book also offers much to the pure turner. A second objective is to offer advice on buying, maintaining, modifying, and repairing lathes. A good part of the book is devoted to the intricacies of lathes and their accessories.

I grew up at the lathe, and I've been turning both wood and metal since I was 12 years old. I understand lathes and how they work. For many years, my father and I owned a company that produced a lathe we codesigned—the Conover Lathe. An outgrowth of our lathe-manufacturing business is Conover Workshops, a woodworking school that my wife and I now run year-round. In 24 years of running the school, I've taught hundreds of people to turn and have a fair sense of where the hurdles are in the learning process.

It's my firm belief that most people have the ability to turn, but this skill has been buried deep inside during the process of growing up. In many cases, it has been masked by fear and dull tools. If you read through the next 180 or so pages, I think you'll be able to regain your instinctive turning skill and have some fun in the process. I look forward to this book starting a revolution in your workshop.

1

The Turning Machine

Woodturning is the art of shaping a rotating piece of wood by the application of sharp tools. The machine that holds and rotates the wood is a lathe. The woodturning lathe is a simple workshop tool that can greatly expand your woodworking horizon. If you want to shape table legs, chair spindles, and bedposts or add embellishments to your furniture in the form of drawer pulls, cabinet knobs, and finials, then you need a lathe. And if you want to make bowls, plates, stool seats, tabletops, and lidded boxes, a lathe is an indispensable machine.

In spindle turning, the grain of the wood being turned runs between the centers of the lathe, that is, parallel to the axis of the lathe (see the illustration on the facing page). You would spindle-turn table legs, porch columns, and chair rungs. In faceplate turning, however, the grain of the work runs at right angles to the axis of the lathe. You would faceplate-turn large drawer pulls and bowls.

Most lathes are supplied with basic chucks—a set of centers and a faceplate. Some people mistakenly think the type of turning is dictated by the type of chuck used to hold the work. For example, many woodworkers associate turning between centers with spindle turning, but it's possible to hold work between centers and yet be faceplate turning. Similarly, it's possible to spindle-turn while having a piece screwed onto a faceplate. (The screws in this case would be into the end grain of the wood.) The important thing to remember is that the orientation of the grain, not how the work is held, dictates whether you are spindle or faceplate turning. It is imperative to understand this distinction because each type of work requires different tools and turning techniques, as you shall see in chapter 4. In fact, using spindle tools for faceplate work can be dangerous.

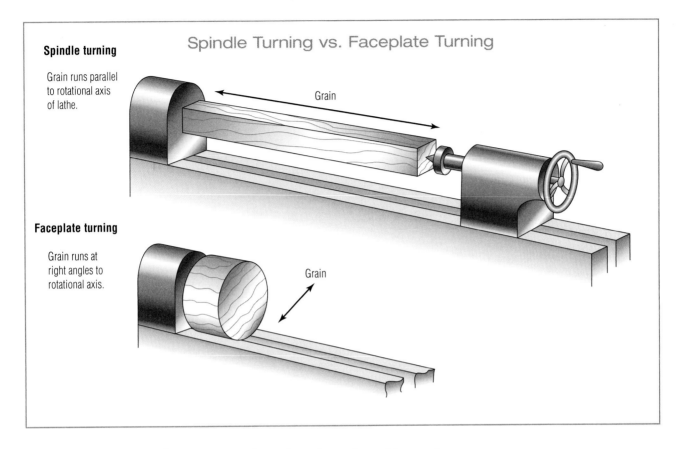

Spindle turning

Grain runs parallel to rotational axis of lathe.

Spindle Turning vs. Faceplate Turning

Grain

Faceplate turning

Grain runs at right angles to rotational axis.

Grain

Lathes range in size from gigantic industrial machines for architectural turning to Lilliputian lathes for turning pens and dollhouse furniture. Knowing about the construction and anatomy will help you choose the right lathe and get it to work more effectively. The type of lathe you need will depend to a large extent on the kind of work (and the amount of turning) you plan to do. For example, if you occasionally want to turn a few chair legs, a light-duty lathe would be more than adequate, whereas heavy bowl turning would require a much sturdier and larger machine. However, there are certain desirable features you should look for in any lathe, so I've drawn attention to these throughout this section to help you make an intelligent buying decision (see chapter 2 for more on choosing a lathe).

Lathe Construction

The earliest lathes were made of wood, and the use of wood as a bed material has survived to the present (I designed and turn on such a lathe). More commonly today, though, lathes are made with all-metal parts. You're likely to encounter several lathe-construction materials: cast iron, fabricated steel, steel stampings, cast aluminum, cast zinc, and extruded aluminum. I have not mentioned plastic here because it is not yet used in major structural components; rather it is reserved for handles, knobs, and housings.

THE LATHE IS ONE OF THE OLDEST complex tools known to man, but determining an exact date of its invention is impossible. The first lathes were undoubtedly spring-pole or bow lathes that were powered by the operator. On a typical spring-pole lathe, the work was held between a set of "dead" centers, which were merely metal points (see the drawing on the facing page). Except for these two metal points, the rest of the lathe was wood.

The bed of the lathe consisted of two stout timbers. On this was mounted a set of "poppits," which carried the dead center points. A rope was attached to a tree branch above the lathe, wrapped several times around the work, and attached to a lever arm that the turner moved up and down with his foot. Cutting was only accomplished on the down stroke, the tree branch providing a mild spring to return the rope for another power stroke.

Later, during medieval times, the pole lathe was brought inside, and the tree branch was replaced with a long bow mounted above the lathe. The rather powerful bow had two strings that passed through off-center holes in a large wood spool onto which the rope was wound. Stepping down on the lever arm turned the work, wound the spool, and compressed the bow. The bow then turned the spool in the opposite direction, revolving the work backward and returning the lever arm to the up position.

A later bow lathe replaced the tree branch and rope with a small bow. The bow was grasped by the operator and seesawed back and forth. Unless a helper could be found, the operator had to hold the tool with one hand. In India, Afghanistan, and Southeast Asia, it is still common to see workers using bow lathes on the ground and guiding the tools with their toes and left hands while they work the bows with their right.

These early lathes could only turn between centers because poppits carried immovable, or dead, centers. Modern lathes came about when the left-hand poppit was given a rotating, or live, spindle and the right poppit was given a retracting spindle. Thus, the headstock and tailstock were born. Needless to say, the headstock also made modern faceplate turning possible.

The first live spindle was nothing more than a steel spindle that fit precisely bored holes in each end of a cast-iron frame. These were called plane bearings. In the 19th century, plane bearings gave way to babbitt, ball, and roller bearings.

These innovations made possible the construction of the great-wheel lathe. In this type of lathe, a pulley on the headstock spindle was belted to a large, or great, wheel 4 ft. to 10 ft. dia. The great-wheel lathe was a direct product of the guild system, under which apprentices or slaves would turn the wheels. Later, water, steam, and gasoline provided the muscle, allowing the great wheel to be replaced by an overhead shaft.

Of great concern to turners is the amount of vibration inherent in a lathe. Any turning convention will find turners waxing lyrical about how quiet and vibration-free their pet lathes are. Any machine has a natural frequency of vibration when given an impulse from a variety of sources such as the motor, work by the operator, or in the case of lathes the work itself. The natural frequency of vibration is the frequency at which the machine will continue to vibrate after an initial impulse, regardless of the source. This frequency is directly proportional to the stiffness of the building material and inversely proportional to mass. This means that the stiffer the material, the higher the frequency, but the more massive the machine, the lower the frequency. The old adage that "you can't beat a good heavy machine" is undoubtedly true.

CAST IRON

Cast iron is a time-honored material for lathe construction that's still hard to beat. The inherent mass of cast iron combined with a favorable modulus of vibration makes for a sweet-running machine. Most woodworking

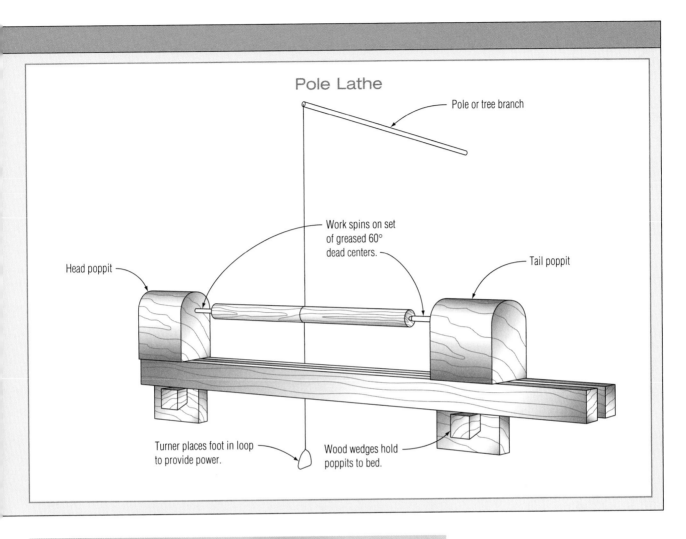

Pole Lathe

Pole or tree branch

Work spins on set of greased 60° dead centers.

Head poppit

Tail poppit

Turner places foot in loop to provide power.

Wood wedges hold poppits to bed.

Most machines come with a 12-in. rest, which is fine for most turning situations.

machinery is cast from grade-25 gray iron, which has a nice balance between strength, damping effect, and machinability. Castings require expensive tooling in the form of patterns, and the casting process itself is expensive—especially in small lots.

Top-quality lathes are made with a heavy cast-iron headstock, tail-stock, and tool-rest assembly. In the past, the bed would also have been cast iron, but today makers are increasingly turning to fabricated structural steel as the bed material.

A lathe with cast-iron major components mounted on a wooden bed is known as a "High Wycombe lathe," so named after the lathes that were popular with turners who turned furniture parts around High Wycombe, England, until the early part of the 20th century. Many of the photographs in this book are of a High Wycombe lathe that I codesigned.

The best economy lathes are often made with cast-iron parts, but the castings are light in keeping with the lathe. On more expensive lathes, the castings are "filled"—a substance not unlike auto body filler is squeegeed on the castings—before painting, resulting in a much better paint job. This difference is purely cosmetic but does reflect the attitude of the manufacturer, just as a better car has a better finish.

FABRICATED STEEL

Fabricated lathes are made by welding together pieces of structural steel. Fabrication first became popular in the late 1950s as a less-expensive alternative to cast-iron castings. Its biggest advantage is that little or no tooling

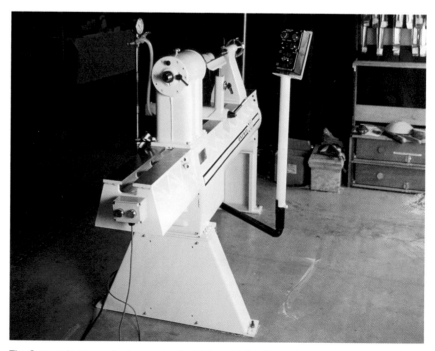

The Oneway is an excellent example of a high-end lathe that makes extensive use of fabricated structural steel in its manufacture.

cost is required, which makes fabrication particularly well suited to small production runs where amortizing the costs of patterns for castings would be difficult. While traditional machine-design theory holds that steel has poor damping qualities compared with grade-25 cast iron, that's only part of the story. It is true that the stiffness of steel makes for high-frequency vibration, but the welds tend to act as barriers to the transmission of vibration. Instead they act much like a cracked glass, stopping vibration. Fabrication is used in both the most expensive and the cheapest lathes, so use common sense when making buying decisions.

STEEL STAMPINGS

Steel stampings are made by placing sheet steel between male and female dies mounted in a press. The press closes the dies on the sheet steel and forms it into the desired shape. Complicated shapes often entail a progression of dies. The cost of the dies for stamping parts can be considerable, but the stamping process itself (unlike foundry work) is cheap. This makes traditional stampings great for high-production work but expensive for short-run work. The last decade has seen the introduction of computer numeric machines that can do short-run stamping on a cost-effective basis. These machines can "nibble" out the basic shape with small round or square dies, then form the material on various standard-forming dies. A stamping made from heavy-gauge metal can be very good, but the most charitable thing that can be said about stampings from light-gauge material is that they are vibration prone. Stampings are used extensively for machine stands, belt covers, and the like.

CAST ALUMINUM AND ZINC

Parts such as pulleys, knobs, and handwheels are often made from cast aluminum or zinc. These are often called die castings because the low melting temperature of aluminum and zinc allows them to be cast in metal molds or dies. Die castings are almost perfect directly from the mold and require little machining. The low weight of aluminum makes it a good material for pulleys because balancing is less of a problem than with cast-iron pulleys. Die-cast knobs and levers are a much better option than plastic.

EXTRUDED ALUMINUM

Occasionally lathes are made of extruded aluminum. Although extrusions can be tempered, the alloys used for the process are soft and gummy. This softness, as well as the tendency of raw aluminum to turn anything it touches black, is somewhat lessened by anodizing, a plating process that puts a thin, hard coat of aluminum oxide on the surface of the metal. However, dents that go through the anodized surface into the soft aluminum substrate are a potential problem.

There are more and more extrusions being used in woodworking machinery today—my table saw fence is an extrusion, for example. Although extrusions are acceptable for miniature lathes and parts of

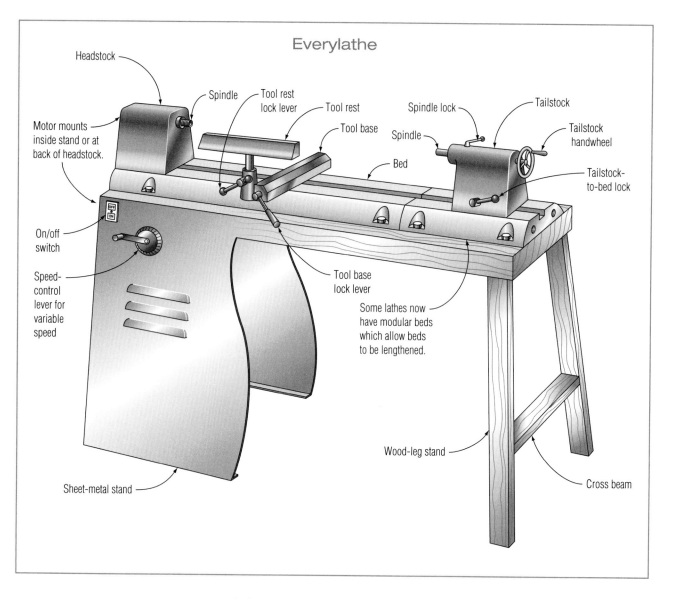

Everylathe

Headstock

Motor mounts inside stand or at back of headstock.

Spindle

Tool rest lock lever

Tool rest

Tool base

Spindle

Spindle lock

Tailstock

Tailstock handwheel

Bed

Tailstock-to-bed lock

On/off switch

Speed-control lever for variable speed

Tool base lock lever

Some lathes now have modular beds which allow beds to be lengthened.

Wood-leg stand

Sheet-metal stand

Cross beam

lathes, I'm not convinced that they are suitable for an entire full-sized machine. Before you buy a lathe made principally of extrusions, consider how much and what type of use you intend for the machine.

HYBRID DESIGNS

Most lathes available today are hybrid designs, incorporating two or more of the construction materials outlined above. A common design is a cast-iron headstock, tailstock, and tool base mounted on a structural-steel bed or, on economy lathes, on solid- or hollow-steel tubing. Steel stampings, sheet metal, aluminum extrusions, and plastic are often used for stands, belt covers, and knobs.

Lathe Anatomy

Lathes come in all makes and sizes, from benchtop models to industrial heavyweights, but the basic design is the same on all lathes. A rigid bed supports a stationary headstock and a tailstock that can be moved to accommodate wood blanks of various lengths. A motor turns a spindle mounted in the headstock, which in turn drives the work. The illustration on the facing page shows a composite woodturning lathe combining the features of many lathes. I call this lathe "Everylathe" because there is probably no lathe that would have all of the features shown—at least at an affordable price. Let's look at the parts in detail.

THE BED

The lathe bed supports the headstock, tailstock, and tool-rest assembly and is in turn supported by a stand. The earliest lathe beds were no more than two wood planks, and wood is still used on some modern lathes. Wood has much to recommend itself as a bed material—it is relatively inexpensive, readily available, absorbs vibration, and can yield a lathe of any desired length between centers. The springiness of a timber bed has shock-absorbing characteristics unmatched by metal.

Starting in the 18th century, cast-iron lathe beds began to displace wood. Cast iron is a good bed material because it is stable and has excellent vibration-damping characteristics. The casting process allows beds of intricate design to be made. In an iron bed, each of the wood planks is replaced by a strip, or rib, which is called a "way." The bed ways are typically 1 in. to 1½ in. apart. A number of lathes today offer modular cast-

A number of lathes offer modular beds so that any reasonable length between centers is possible. This Nova 3000 has 20-in. sections.

iron beds (see the photo on p. 11). Under this scheme, the standard package gives the turner a decent distance between centers, but additional sections (typically 12 in. to 20 in. long) can be added to achieve a bed of any reasonable length.

Although structural steel does not have the damping ability of cast iron, it makes a good, solid bed if the weldments are designed properly. Steel also makes longer beds possible at reasonable cost. You can even make a "stretched" structural-steel bed by obtaining lengths of matching steel from a steel fabricator.

I've seen two lathes with beds made from aluminum extrusions. Extrusions don't have much to offer as a bed material for anything but a miniature lathe, so I would avoid them on a full-sized lathe.

In a bed, you should look for rigidity and workmanship. The ways should have a smooth surface, and the distance between them should be constant. Make sure the tailstock and tool base slide easily but lock solid where you put them. Test the truth of the bed by checking the alignment of the headstock and tailstock (see the sidebar on p. 23).

THE HEADSTOCK

The business end of any lathe—the part that drives the work—is the headstock assembly. The headstock is fixed permanently at the left end of the bed and consists of either a casting, a welded steel body, or an extrusion that holds a spindle set in bearings. A pulley on the spindle is con-

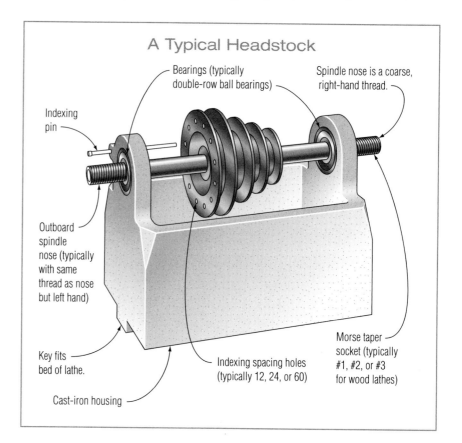

A Typical Headstock

Bearings (typically double-row ball bearings)

Spindle nose is a coarse, right-hand thread.

Indexing pin

Outboard spindle nose (typically with same thread as nose but left hand)

Key fits bed of lathe.

Cast-iron housing

Indexing spacing holes (typically 12, 24, or 60)

Morse taper socket (typically #1, #2, or #3 for wood lathes)

STANDARD SPINDLE SIZES AND MORSE TAPERS

Spindle thread size	Manufacturer	Morse taper	
		Headstock	Tailstock
⅝ in. plain (unthreaded)	Shopsmith	None	#2
¾ in. x 16 TPI*	Sears, Coronet, Record, Beaver	None or #1	None or #1
⅞ in. x 14 TPI	Rockwell Homecraft	#1	#1
1 in. x 8 TPI	Delta and many others (most common spindle size)	#2	#2
1 in. x 12 TPI**	Myford	#2	#2
1⅛ in. x 8 TPI	Oliver	#2	#2
1¼ in. x 8 TPI	General, Nova, Woodfast, Vicmarc	#2	#2
M33 x 3.5mm (with locking groove)	Oneway	#2	#3
1½ in. x 8 TPI	Conover, Powermatic, Atlas, South Bend	#2 or #3	#2
1½ in. x 6 TPI	Union Graduate (Harrison)	#2	#2
*TPI = threads per inch **Whitworth thread (54° flank angle, rather than 60°)			

nected by a belt to a motor, which is normally mounted below or behind the headstock (see the illustration on the facing page).

Spindle The spindle, a threaded shaft mounted horizontally, is the heart of the headstock. It accepts the drive centers, faceplates, and other accessories that hold and power the work. Spindles are either hollow or solid and range in size from ½ in. to 1½ in. dia.

The spindle size you need depends on the type of turning you intend to do. For turning spindles between centers, you can get by with a small-diameter spindle. A common spindle size that is adequate for medium-duty work is 1 in. For heavy-duty faceplate turning and architectural turning, you will need at least a 1¼-in. spindle that will not flex under load. Watch out for spindles with odd thread sizes or odd taper sizes—what may seem like a bargain will be no bargain at all if you can't easily obtain accessories to fit the spindle. The chart above lists common spindle sizes for which you have a good chance of readily finding accessories.

You should give much consideration to the spindle when choosing a lathe. The most important thing to look for is a hollow spindle that is machined to accept Morse-taper accessories. Morse tapers lock in place when inserted into the matching tapered socket in the spindle.

More than any other feature, Morse tapers separate good lathes from bad. Even if your turning needs are very casual, the advantages of Morse

LATHE SIZE IS TYPICALLY specified in three ways, the first two of which are closely related. The first measurement is center height—the distance between the point of a drive center in the spindle and the top of the bed—which determines the diameter of the work that the lathe can accommodate. The second measurement is swing, which is double the center height of the lathe. For standard spindle turning between centers, a center height of 4 in. (yielding a swing of 8 in.) is adequate. For heavy-duty bowl turning, a center height of at least 6 in. is desirable.

The third measurement of lathe size is the maximum distance obtainable between the headstock and tailstock centers. This capacity determines the maximum length of work that can be turned. For spindle turning, 30 in. is the absolute minimum and 36 in. or more is preferable.

tapers are enormous. A Morse-taper socket in the spindle makes for quick and easy mounting of drive centers and a host of other chucking accessories. Morse tapers lock when driven home and release with an equal opposite force. They're universal, so you're not dependent on the manufacturer for replacement accessories. By contrast, on a lathe that has a solid spindle, all accessories have to be screwed on, which is not only time-consuming but also limits the range of accessories available and ties you to the manufacturer.

Morse tapers are available in sizes #0 through #7 (see the chart below for the sizes common to wood lathes). They have been widely copied in the forms of other locking tapers, such as the American Standard taper, the British Standard taper, the Brown and Sharps taper, and the Jarno taper. If you come across a used lathe with a taper size that does not appear to be Morse, *Machinery's Handbook* (Industrial Press, 2000) will be a great help. It lists dimensions for all types of locking tapers.

A further consideration is the height of the spindle above the bed, which dictates the swing of the lathe and the diameter of the work that can be turned (see the sidebar above). At its simplest, swing is double the height of the spindle center over the bed. For example, a lathe with a center height of 6 in. will swing 12 in. You have to be careful of manufacturers' claims because they sometimes quote the swing over a "gap," which is a short dip in the bed just ahead of the headstock. This gap,

Look for Morse Tapers

Morse tapers in both the headstock and the tailstock are watershed features that separate serious lathes from bad ones. Avoid purchasing a lathe without Morse tapers.

MORSE-TAPER SIZES

Size	Dia. small end	Dia. large end	Length
#0	0.252 in.	0.356 in.	2¹¹⁄₃₂ in.
#1	0.369 in.	0.475 in.	2⁹⁄₁₆ in.
#2	0.572 in.	0.700 in.	3⅛ in.
#3	0.778 in.	0.938 in.	3⅞ in.

which is typically about 2 in. deep, allows you to turn larger-diameter face-plate work in this area. The problem is that when work extends into the gap you can work only on the face (the exposed side) of it.

Unfortunately, twice the center height above the bed is not a true measure of capacity. A better yardstick is to measure the distance from the top of the tool base to the center of the spindle. Doubling this will give you the true swing, which is the diameter of work the lathe will swing between centers. A lot of faceplate turning also requires placing the tool base under the work.

Bearings Bearings hold the spindle rigidly in place and allow it to turn with a minimum of friction. They're an important consideration when buying a lathe. The problem is that bearings are much harder to judge on cursory examination than features such as the construction method or spindle type.

Historically, lathes have run on plane cast-iron bearings, sleeve bearings, and babbitt bearings (see the illustration on p. 16), but most lathes made today have rolling-element bearings. These include ball, roller, and tapered-roller bearings (see the photo below right). Of these, ball bearings are by far the most common type used in lathe construction. Each bearing

Tool-rest height dramatically affects swing. This tool rest comes from a lathe that advertises a 16-in. swing. The standard tool rest for this Nova 3000 is much higher than the tool rest for a Conover lathe, which yields about 2 in. of extra swing over the rest.

Today most woodturning lathes have at least one set of double-row bearings. Shown here is an SKF angular-contact bearing of the type put in the best machines. (Photo courtesy SKF bearings.)

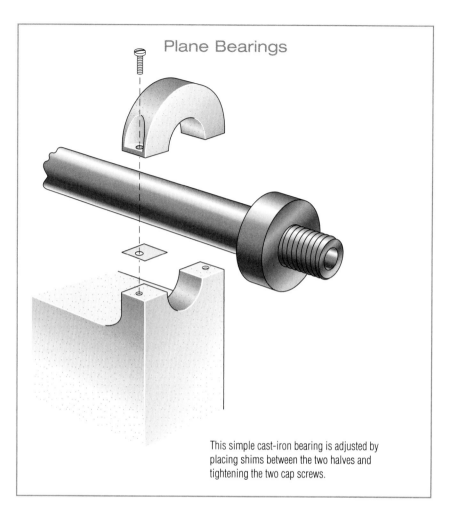

Plane Bearings

This simple cast-iron bearing is adjusted by placing shims between the two halves and tightening the two cap screws.

consists of an inner race and an outer race that are separated by a series of steel balls. The opposing ends of the spindle ride on these rings of balls, which provide a precise hold and allow the spindle to turn with a minimum of effort. The majority of the power from the motor can now be used for productive work.

Bearings can sometimes be upgraded, which I will discuss on pp. 149–155.

Outboard turning feature Because some work will be too large in diameter to swing over the bed, lathe manufacturers often design the headstock so that work can be mounted on the outboard side. Outboard turning is accomplished in two basic ways. One is to put a left-hand thread on the outboard end of the headstock spindle and mount the work so that it faces away from the lathe. The other option is to design the headstock so that it pivots at right angles to the bed.

When work is mounted on the outboard end of the headstock, the swing of the lathe becomes double the distance from the center of the headstock spindle to the floor. Although this may sound like an ideal solution for turning large-diameter work, outboard turning presents a number of problems, the greatest of which is speed. Many lathes do not have a low enough speed range to turn anything greater than 12 in. in diameter. For large-diameter turning, you need a bottom speed of 150 rpm to 300 rpm.

Another problem with outboard turning is that there is no place to support the tool rest. You have to use a floor-stand rest (typically a tripod stand that holds the rest), but this device is not as solid as a standard rest. In addition, this method of outboard turning sometimes requires a second set of left-hand-threaded faceplates, and it demands that you do everything in reverse of your normal way of turning. (Delta makes many of its faceplates threaded in both directions, which means they can be screwed on either end of the spindle.)

Some lathes that use the outboard end of the spindle for outboard turning have a special tool base attached rigidly to the lathe, which is a much better setup. In effect, this creates a small bowl lathe that is a mirror image of the actual lathe.

The second option for outboard turning, the swing-head design, is well adapted to light- and medium-duty lathes. In a swing-head lathe, the headstock pivots at right angles, and the work is turned in front of the lathe (see the photo at left on p. 18). A special tool base attaches to the base of the headstock into which the tool rest fits. Although such a setup allows only a limited outboard swing of about 16 in. to 20 in., it's a better arrangement for a number of reasons. First, the diameter of the work is limited to within the low-speed range of the lathe. Second, the tool base is attached rigidly to the lathe bed, making turning sure and safe. Third,

A floor-stand rest allows outboard turning, but you must have a lathe with low enough speed to handle this kind of diameter.

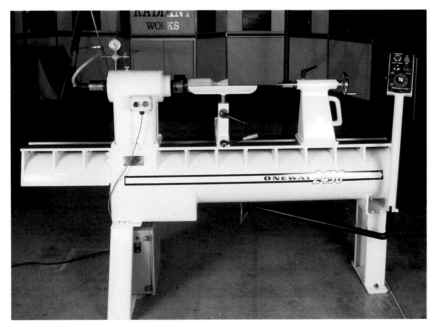

Oneway offers a short bed that can be mounted outboard (opposite the standard bed that comes with the machine), which turns the machine into a bowl lathe. This offers great convenience to a serious bowl turner because he has much better access.

Most manufacturers of today's light- and medium-duty lathes handle outboard turning by allowing the head to pivot. This gives reasonable outboard capability without having to go to a floor-stand rest or buy left-hand faceplates.

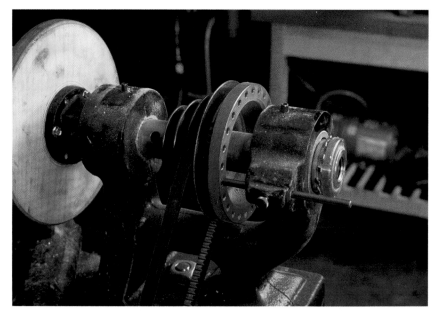

Indexing allows the locking of the headstock spindle at precise locations for purposes of layout (such as a clock face), hand operations (carving flutes), or machine operations (milling reeds with a router). Most manufacturers offer at least 12 positions, with 24 or 60 being the common numbers.

turning is in the same direction and orientation as takes place over the bed. Finally, a second set of left-hand-threaded faceplates is not required.

It has been my experience both in selling lathes and advising buyers of lathes that turners place unnecessary emphasis on turning outboard. In reality, outboard turning is something that most people will do only once or twice in their lifetimes, if at all. Don't have tunnel vision about the outboard feature, ignoring all the other useful features that a lathe should have and that you will use every turning session. You can always rig something up or borrow a lathe for the once-in-a-lifetime big job.

Index heads Some headstocks are fitted with an index head, which is a mechanism that allows the spindle to be locked at equal intervals so that layout or auxiliary operations can be performed. Examples of such applications include laying out a clock face or a fluting pattern on a bowl or milling reeds or flutes in a column with a router (see pp. 102–104). The most common setup for indexing is a series of holes drilled in the headstock drive pulley (see the photo above right), which is mounted on the spindle. A pin in the headstock casting slides into the appropriate hole and locks the spindle in place. Common hole patterns are 12, 24, and 60. I like the 24-stop configuration because it allows me to divide the circumference of a workpiece into many different but equal sets of parts: 24 (for fluted bowls and the like), 12 (for clock faces), 8 (common for period-furniture shapes), 6 (also for furniture), and 3 (I have never used this).

Indexing is a feature that may or may not be of value to you. I have spoken to many turners who have never used the index head. For certain types of period-furniture turning, such as fluted legs, it is essential. If you are considering a dandy lathe at a bargain price but it lacks indexing, buy it anyway. An index head can be added later if you need it. There are several after-market chucks that incorporate the feature, or you can rig something up yourself. Note that on most lathes the index head should not be used as a spindle lock for removing faceplates because doing so may bend the indexing stop. Most lathes have other provisions for locking the spindle for faceplate removal.

MOTORS, BELTS, AND PULLEYS

Almost all woodworking lathes are supplied with a single-phase induction motor. The motor typically mounts inside the stand or at the back of the headstock and is connected to a pulley on the spindle by a belt. For small lathes, ½ hp is adequate, whereas bigger machines require 1 hp or even 1½ hp. Mini lathes can get by with as little as ¼ hp. Machines imported from Asia frequently have power specifications on the motor nameplates that are optimistic. Often such machines are quite serviceable otherwise, so the best course is to replace the anemic motor with a U.S. model if it lacks the desired power or burns out.

Increasingly, manufacturers are putting variable-speed direct-current (DC) and alternating-current (AC) motors with solid-state controllers on lathes. Today's solid-state circuitry allows the use of controllers that effi-

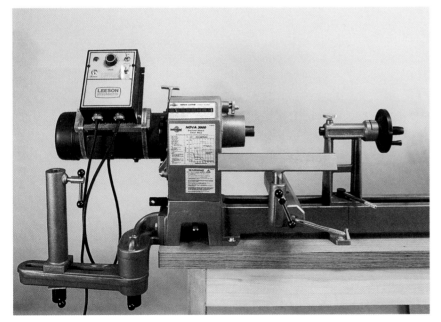

A DC motor is a nice way to add variable speed to an existing lathe. Many manufacturers now offer DC (or variable-cycle-rate AC) as the method of variable speed.

Adding Variable Speed

The easiest way to add variable speed to an older machine is to install a DC motor and controller or a three-phase AC motor and a solid-state variable-cycle rate controller.

ciently make DC current from ordinary single-phase household current. This makes it possible simply to dial a speed, which is much more convenient than having to move a belt by hand to change speed. Such a controller cannot be used with a standard induction motor; it requires a DC motor. DC variable speed requires both a controller and a DC motor.

For variable-speed AC, a solid-state single-phase controller is attached to a standard three-phase motor. The controller takes your 60-cycle single-phase electrical house (or shop) current and delivers three-phase current at an any cycle rate between about 2 and 65 cycles. The speed of AC induction motors is controlled by the cycle rate of the current, so slowing the cycle rate slows the motor. With this system, the motor is inexpensive but the controller is about the same price as a DC motor and controller combined.

Either AC or DC solid-state controllers work beautifully and are my preferred form of power. The drawback to both AC and DC variable-speed power is cost. They are expensive—$500 and up. Still they offer the easiest (and often the cheapest) way to add variable speed to a lathe that does not have this feature.

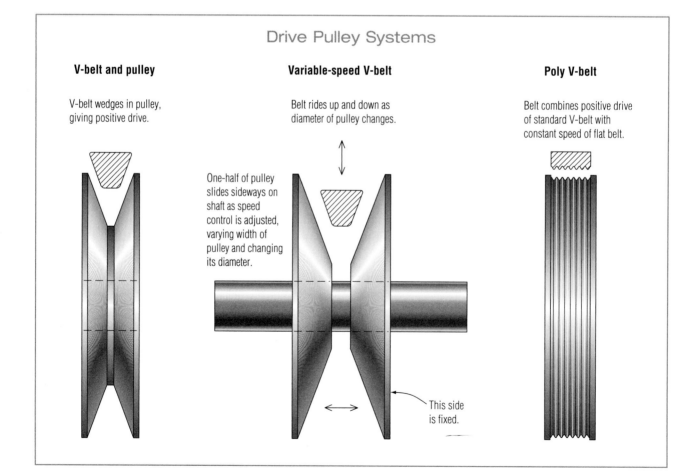

Drive Pulley Systems

V-belt and pulley

V-belt wedges in pulley, giving positive drive.

Variable-speed V-belt

Belt rides up and down as diameter of pulley changes.

One-half of pulley slides sideways on shaft as speed control is adjusted, varying width of pulley and changing its diameter.

This side is fixed.

Poly V-belt

Belt combines positive drive of standard V-belt with constant speed of flat belt.

The original drive system for connecting lathes to a power source was a flat leather belt. A three- or four-step set of matched pulleys gave a good range of speeds for the turner. Although flat leather belts gave very constant speed with no surging, they tended to slip, thus wasting power.

Most lathes made in recent years use V-belts for power transmission. V-belts drive positively because greater tension on the belt causes it to wedge tighter in the pulley groove. An additional advantage of V-belts is that manufacturers can provide variable speed by installing a variable-width pulley set (see the illustration on the facing page). A mechanical control adjusts the width of the drive pulley, which effectively changes the pulley diameter and thus the speed. Moving the two halves of the drive pulley apart decreases the diameter (and decreases the speed); squeezing the halves back together does the reverse.

The mating pulley on the headstock is similarly split but is spring-loaded so it automatically adjusts to the state of the drive pulley. This setup gives a wide range of infinitely variable speeds. The only drawback to such a speed-control system is that it wears out belts faster, necessitating annual belt replacement for a lathe that gets moderate to heavy use.

A recent innovation is the poly V-belt, which is a flat rubber belt with a series of small V-ribs machined on the inside surface (see the illustration on the facing page). This design gives the belt the positive drive characteristics of a V-belt with the constant velocity of a flat leather belt. Many newer lathes run on poly V-belts.

THE TAILSTOCK

The tailstock assembly is composed of the main casting, a spindle (or ram), a spindle-locking lever, a handwheel, and a mechanism to secure the unit to the lathe bed. Whereas the headstock is stationary, the tailstock can slide along the bed to accommodate work of varying lengths and can be locked at the desired distance from the headstock.

The advantages of a good tailstock should not be overlooked because it does much more than just hold a center. As with the headstock spindle, the tailstock spindle should be machined to accept Morse-taper accessories. Look for a spindle equipped with a #1, #2, or #3 Morse taper. The tailstock spindle sometimes runs a bit smaller than the headstock spindle. For example, if the headstock spindle is 1½ in. dia., the tailstock spindle is typically 1 in.

An important aspect of tailstock design is spindle travel—the amount the spindle can be moved when the tailstock is locked to the bed. Lathes typically have about 2½ in. of spindle travel, which is adequate for most applications. I prefer to work with a tailstock spindle that can move as much as possible because the tailstock itself doesn't have to be moved as often.

The tailstock spindle is advanced and withdrawn by turning a handwheel, which is no more than a large nut. A lever on top of the tailstock locks the spindle in place and prevents it from drifting due to the vibra-

A common tailstock design uses a left-hand thread on the outside of the spindle. The left-hand thread is necessary to make the adjustment logical—turning the handwheel right advances the spindle and vice versa. This also allows a hollow spindle for drilling through the tailstock.

tion caused by turning. The traditional tailstock setup calls for the outside of the spindle to be left-hand threaded (see the photo on p. 21). Because the thread is left-handed, the spindle advances when the handwheel is turned clockwise, which is normal to our way of thinking. This design is typically used on cheaper lathes, although it is sometimes also found on very expensive ones. Accessories are ejected by inserting a knockout bar through the spindle.

A more elegant arrangement is a self-ejecting spindle. The inside of the spindle is left-hand threaded, and a long left-hand screw extends from the handwheel into it (see the photo below). Turning the wheel to the right advances the spindle, while turning it left withdraws it. As the spindle is retracted all the way rearward, the screw bumps the Morse taper in the spindle and ejects it. A crank handle is often added to the handwheel so that the spindle can be moved quickly.

The tailstock must lock securely to the bed and not move while you're turning. There is a variety of locking mechanisms, ranging from a stud running down between the bed rails with a plate and a nut to complicated cams. The main thing to look for is a good positive lock that will hold the tailstock without its drifting backward when you apply pressure to the work with the handwheel.

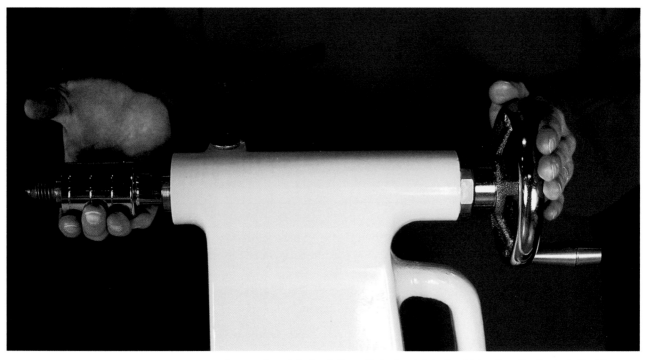

A more elegant design is the self-ejecting tailstock, which automatically ejects the Morse taper in the spindle when the spindle is fully withdrawn. You cannot drill through such spindles, however.

WHEN YOU BUY A NEW LATHE, it's a good idea to check that the tailstock aligns with the headstock. (This test will also check the truth of the bed.) The best gauge for testing center alignment is a pair of 60° dead centers (see pp. 43–45), but any set of Morse-taper accessories that come to a point at the center will work. Simply put one center in the tailstock and one center in the headstock, then slide the tailstock forward until the two points touch. The centers should align perfectly.

Center alignment is important in faceplate work but relatively unimportant for spindle turning. Although reasonable center alignment is advantageous (if for no other reason than that the tool rest aligns with the work), center alignment could vary by ⅛ in. or more on a 15-in. spindle. The longer the turning, the more out of alignment the two centers could be. Center alignment is especially important if you plan to do any metal spinning with your lathe. Woodcraft Supply Corp. sells a clever double-ended #2 Morse taper for checking spindle alignment, as shown above.

THE TOOL BASE AND TOOL REST

What we tend to think of as the tool rest is actually composed of two parts—the tool-base assembly and the tool rest itself. The tool base, which supports the tool rest, attaches to the bed of the lathe and can slide to any point between the headstock and the tailstock. The base (known as the banjo in England) also moves in and out so that the tool rest can be positioned right next to the workpiece. Desirable features in a tool base include ease of movement, rigidity, and a low profile. The latter feature is important because the height of the base affects the swing of the lathe. For each ⅛ in. that the tool-base height is reduced, you are rewarded with an extra ¼ in. of swing.

The tool base must lock down securely and not slide under load. The hold-down/locking mechanisms range from wedges under the bed that are pounded snug with a mallet on classic wood-bed machines to a simple nut and bolt that are tightened with a wrench on economy lathes to complicated lever-operated cam mechanisms on full-featured machines. With each level of sophistication come commensurate increases in price. When choosing a lathe, the best course is to try the tool base to see how it operates. Move it to a variety of angles and positions, lock it in place, grab it with both hands, and see if you can move it. Don't be afraid to throw some body weight into this exercise.

A full-length wood rest works just fine for turning long stair balusters.

The tool rest provides a fulcrum point for support and control of tools during turning. The rest mounts in the tool base and is adjustable to any height and angle. A locking mechanism (ranging from a simple knob and stud to a cam) secures the rest in the tool base. The front surface of the rest should have sufficient slope so that any tool will contact only the top edge in any turning operation.

The tool rest should be of solid construction. Cast iron is the traditional material, but structural steel performs just as well and wood may also be used. Lathe manufacturers offer tool rests in standard lengths of 6 in., 12 in., 18 in., and 36 in., but sometimes the longer rests require two tool bases. For special turning situations, you can have a local welder fabricate a longer rest from structural steel, or you can make your own full-length tool rest out of wood (see the illustration on the facing page).

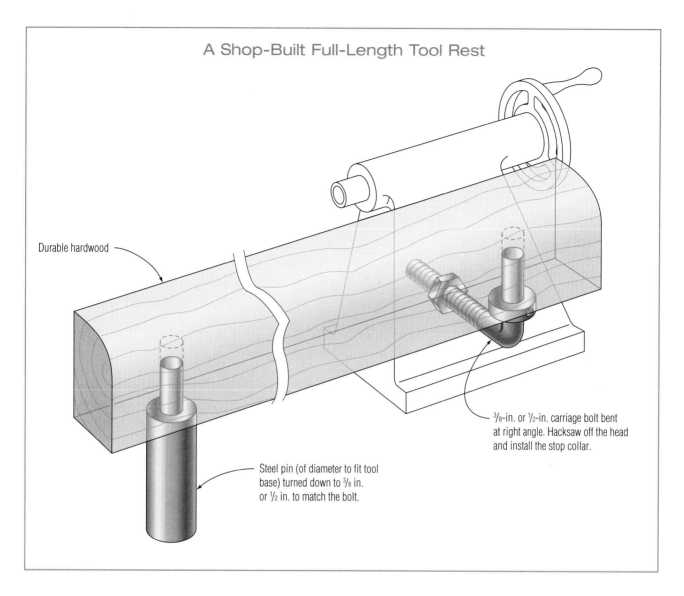

A Shop-Built Full-Length Tool Rest

Durable hardwood

3/8-in. or 1/2-in. carriage bolt bent at right angle. Hacksaw off the head and install the stop collar.

Steel pin (of diameter to fit tool base) turned down to 3/8 in. or 1/2 in. to match the bolt.

THE STAND

When choosing a lathe, it's important to look for a solid stand that will prevent the lathe from jumping around under full load. Nineteenth- and early 20th-century lathes typically had heavy cast-iron legs (weighing as much as 300 lb.) that minimized vibration. The legs were usually bolted to the end of the bed, which made for a freestanding machine that you could stand close to without stubbing your toes.

Today, cast-iron legs have largely been replaced by stamped-sheet-metal stands. By using angle and box sections, manufacturers can fabricate serviceable stands from light-gauge material. Such stands are inexpensive to make, cut down on shipping weight, and, if shipped knocked down, save on shipping volume. A well-designed sheet-metal stand can be very good, whereas a poorly designed stand can impair the performance of an otherwise good lathe.

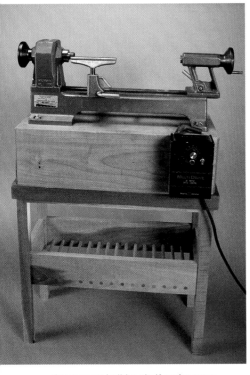

If you must build a shelf under your lathe, use dowels, which allow dust and chips to fall through but not your tools and accessories.

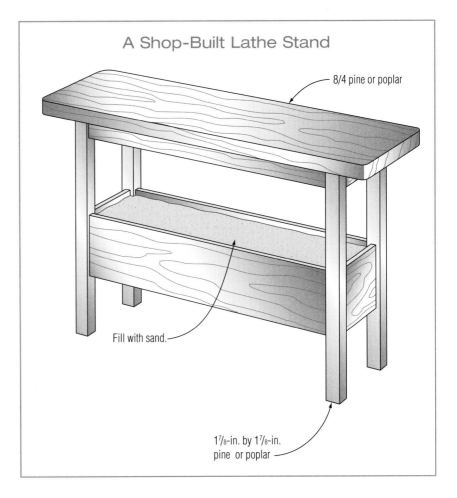

A Shop-Built Lathe Stand

8/4 pine or poplar

Fill with sand.

$1\frac{7}{8}$-in. by $1\frac{7}{8}$-in. pine or poplar

Some economy lathes are sold with the stand as an option. These stands are invariably of poor quality, and you're much better off building your own stand (see the illustration above). Building box sections and filling them with sand will give you a base that soaks up vibration and cuts down on lathe noise. Wood is stronger and more rigid than a light stamped-steel stand. I built the stand for my Nova 3000 (see the photo on p. 30) from heavy hardwood. The tapered-leg design increases stability, and the shelf can accept sandbags if necessary.

Avoid shelves and drawers under your lathe unless they are made of dowels or bars; otherwise they tend to fill with chips and collect dust. By making a shelf with dowels, the chips will fall through. I prefer a lathe with legs on either end rather than a box underneath so as to make sweeping and shoveling chips much easier.

Choosing and Buying a Lathe

Today, a lathe buyer is presented with a startling array of lathes. A happy outgrowth of 21st century instant communication, the woodworking press, and local turning clubs is that there are far fewer really bad lathes out there. That is because manufacturers (and the woodworking public) hear fast when something is wrong. In addition to new lathes, however, there are lots of used lathes kicking around that are begging for loving parents to adopt them. The used lathe represents one of the best options for a buyer on a tight budget. In chapter 7, I give ample information on repairing and refurbishing a previously owned lathe. Restoring the classic beauty of an old warhorse only adds to the fun of using it.

Before beginning your search, you need to analyze the type and amount of turning you plan to do with your lathe. For example, if you plan to make dollhouse furniture, a miniature lathe is the right bet. If, on the other hand, you plan for the lathe to be only an adjunct to your general furniture making, you can get by with a modest lathe. Almost any lathe can handle chair legs, table legs, knobs, and pulls.

However, if you are a serious period furniture maker and wish to do chairs with long back posts and Sheridan bedposts, you will need a heavy lathe with good between-center distance, as much as 72 in. You also may wish to make tilt tables, fern stands, and the like, which require good outboard faceplate capacity. If you wish to do really heavy turning, such as architectural elements (porch columns, for example), you will need an even bigger lathe. If you enjoy bowl turning, then you may want to consider a bowl lathe.

LATHE TYPES

Type	Use	Capacity
True miniature lathes	• True miniature turning such as dollhouse furniture	Swing: 4 in. or less Length between centers: 6 in. to 8 in.
Mini lathes (small lathes with a short bed)	• Turning pens • As a second lathe or a portable lathe • Teaching children	Swing: up to 10 in. Length between centers: up to 14 in. Sometimes these lathes have extension beds that turn them into small benchtop lathes.
General turning lathes	• Good general shop lathe for any spindle work up to about 30 in. between centers and general faceplate work 13 in. to 16 in. dia.	Swing: up to 16 in. Length between centers: up to 52 in. but most in the 28-in. to 36-in. range
Bowl lathes	• Turning bowls	Swing: at least 16 in. and often 22 in. or more. Length between centers: not much much more than 24 in.(on a true bowl lathe the tailstock is minimal, meant only to provide support during roughing)
Ornamental lathes (OT lathes)	• OT attachments do end-grain cutting, side-grain cutting, and threading. • True OT lathes do ornamental patterns but are hard to find and expensive.	Capacities are typically modest—no more than 6 in. center height.

How Much Can You Spend?

Decide how much money you have to spend before shopping for a lathe, and remember that you will need at least $150 for some tools and accessories after you purchase your lathe.

Finally, you should decide at the outset how much money you can spend for your lathe. Buying machinery, especially for an enthusiast, can be much like buying a car—budgets get busted. Remember not to spend all your money on the lathe because you also need tools, chucks, and accessories, which can add as much as $150 to $750 to your budget. There are basically three price points in lathes: less than $1,000 (entry-level lathes), less than $2,000 (mid-range lathes), and more than $2,000 (dream lathes). There are also specialty lathes if you concentrate on one type of turning.

At the top end of the market almost any lathe will be satisfactory, but among entry-level lathes it is possible to find virtually unusable examples. Entry-level buyers need to be especially careful. Buying a lathe is much like buying a car; a feature that you love may be a feature that I hate. Before you buy your first lathe, try out the one you're considering.

A turning club is often worth joining because a member may own the lathe you are interested in and be glad to let you try it. The Internet is also a useful resource to find user feedback on any particular machine. On the other hand, I would also caution you against taking other users' comments too much to heart. Typically woodworkers get very comfortable with their lathes and look askance at any machine that is different from what they are used to. If most of the features of a particular lathe appeal to you, don't be afraid if it seems a bit awkward at first. Using it will become second nature within two weeks.

Entry-Level Lathes

Entry-level lathes are suitable for a craftsperson who wants to add turning to his woodworking. They will handle the majority of furniture parts such as table legs, chair legs, knobs, finials, and stool seats. Such lathes typically have about a 10-in. to 14-in. swing (over the bed) with 28 in. to 36 in. between centers. Longer turnings can normally be jointed at one or two places, so you can even tackle period bedposts. Only back posts for ladder-back and rocking chairs present any problem (for these you need 42 in. to 55 in. between centers). Because turners value swing, most entry-level lathes have an ample amount.

New entry-level lathes cost from $500 to $1,000 dollars. But in this category, a used lathe offers a lot of value. The only drawback is that you may not get quite as much swing. On the other hand, you may find a nice old workhorse for the price of a new lathe. During the Depression, a lot of cheap lathes were manufactured with sleeve bearings, but I would stay away from any machine that does not have ball or roller bearings. Likewise, stay away from a machine that does not have Morse-taper sockets in both the headstock and tailstock. Morse tapers are a watershed feature that separates good lathes from not-so-good lathes.

The Delta 46-700 was a groundbreaking lathe when it was introduced in the early 1990s and is still a winner. It offers cast-iron construction where it counts, reasonable swing and between-center distances, and a swing head for larger faceplate work. Best of all, it has variable speed with a low-end speed of 350 rpm. (Photo courtesy Delta.)

Based on the Delta 46-700, this Jet lathe is a good small lathe that offers good swing and between-center distances with a swing head for occasional larger faceplate work.

Most entry-level lathes come with $\frac{1}{2}$-hp motors, although the motors of lathes made in Asia are often a bit optimistic in their power ratings. You can easily replace a motor when the original fails. Typically these lathes come with three or four speeds, which are changed by switching belts, but some entry-level machines have variable speed by variable-width sheaves.

A good entry-level lathe has excellent resale value should you ever decide to upgrade.

Mid-Range Lathes

If you want to turn a lot of furniture parts or even make turning the main focus of your woodworking, then there is probably a mid-range lathe in your future. Mid-range lathes are of much heavier construction than an entry-level machine, although they may not offer vastly more capacity (swing and distance between centers) these days. Along with the heavier construction, you also get better knobs and controls, smoother operation of movable parts, and better power. The motor will be more powerful, typically 1 hp to $1\frac{1}{2}$ hp, and often of better construction. You will also get a bigger selection of speeds or more likely variable speed. In general, the weight and rigidity create a smoother-operating machine that is much less prone to vibration. Mid-range lathes can easily last you a lifetime. They cost from $1,000 to $2,000.

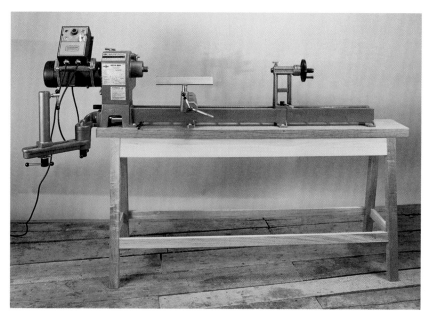

The Nova 3000 is a well-designed, mid-range lathe. It offers all the features of the Delta 46-700 with greater swing, DC power options, and a modular bed design that allows the bed to extend. Nova also builds an ornamental attachment for this lathe.

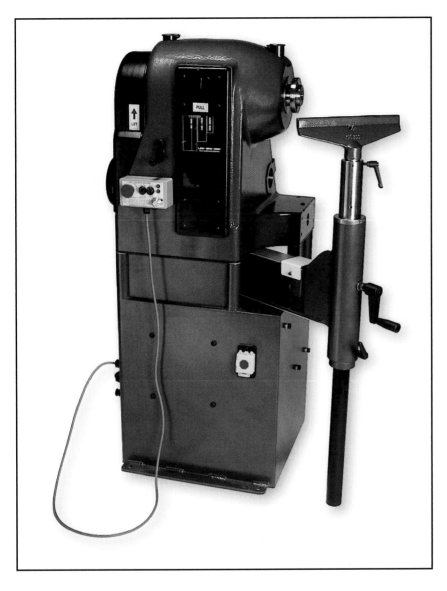

The VB36 Master Bowlturner lathe certainly qualifies as a dream lathe. Made in England, this robust bowl lathe weighs 850 lb. and costs just under $5,000.

Dream Lathes

As the heading implies, these machines have everything you always dreamed about in a lathe. Heavy-duty construction, controls that work effortlessly, trouble-free operation, lots of power at any speed, and nice cosmetics. In short, this is a lathe you will never be ashamed about being seen with in public. New lathes run more than $2,000 and as much as $6,000. Of course, you may luck out and find a beautiful used lathe for much, much less. Also included in this category are special-purpose lathes that have huge swing and tremendous between-center capacity or that do ornamental work. Dream lathes are generally the province of the avid turner who forsakes other types of woodworking. Sure, it's a lot of money, but then have you ever priced golf clubs?

The Carba-Tec is a true miniature lathe
Weighing 36 lb., it is highly portable.

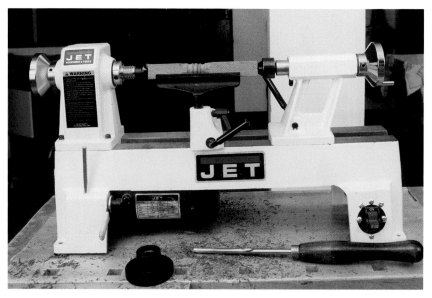

The Jet is typical of today's so-called mini lathes. In reality, it is a short bench lathe with a 10-in. swing and 14 in. between centers. At 78 lb., it is not so portable.

Specialty Lathes

Beyond the general turning lathes are a variety of lathes for more specialized types of turning. You can find pretty much anything you need for whatever area of turning you want to pursue.

MINIATURE LATHES

The theory that you need a small lathe to turn miniatures is just a myth. You need high speed, but you can do such work with full-sized lathes. In fact, a full-sized lathe is the best option for most people because you won't be limited to miniature turning. However, if your work is strictly miniature, then a miniature lathe makes sense because moving the tool rest will be easier and you'll have better access to the work. There are a gaggle of lathes on the market today that are sold as "mini" lathes but are in reality simply short-bedded benchtop lathes.

Such mini lathes are actually not that small. The largest will handle as much as 10-in.-dia. work (over the bed) up to 14 in. long between centers. So a large mini lathe can accommodate small bowls and spindle work up to about the size of a candlestick. True miniature lathes handle work in the 3-in.- to 4-in.-dia. (over the bed) range with 8 in. between centers.

Despite a mini lathe's limitations, the startling array of miniature lathes on the market is a sign of this type of lathe's popularity. These Lilliputian lathes appeal to a big chunk of the turning market. I am convinced that many entry turners buy minis as their first lathes and many ardent turners buy one as their second lathes. They are less daunting, so they make learning basics more enjoyable. They are particularly good if you want to get a child interested in turning. A very nice mini lathe with a variable-speed motor can cost an affordable $300 to $400.

Many avid turners take them to club meetings so that they can actively participate in training sessions. Their portability is wonderful, and they can be stored out of the way when not in use. I use mine whenever I have to turn a bunch of knobs. One summer I spent several enjoyable evenings on my patio turning 40 pulls for a kitchen's cabinets and drawers.

Mini lathes are also very popular with pen makers. Turning wooden mechanical pencils as well as ball, felt-tip, and fountain pens is a huge business these days, and many turning enthusiasts make nice secondary incomes by turning pens. A mini lathe can be dedicated to pens, thus leaving your main lathe open for general turning.

BOWL LATHES

Another specialty lathe is the bowl lathe. Because of the popularity of turning bowls, a number of lathes have been designed with only this end in mind. A bowl lathe has a short bed so that the turner can stand directly in front of the work and walk 180° around it. The tailstock is rudimentary, just holding the work during roughing and secondary operations. These lathes are hard to find and can be expensive. Some manufacturers offer a short cantilevered bed that mounts outboard opposite the main bed, turning the lathe into a bowl lathe.

The Vicmarc is typical of a mini lathe. It is big enough to handle lots of turning but small enough to handle dollhouse furniture-sized components and pens conveniently. I like mine because it is easy to lug to demonstrations.

ORNAMENTAL LATHES

An interesting subgenre of turning that became popular (at least among the wealthy) in the second half of the 19th century was ornamental turning (OT), in which precisely cut decorations are put on turned surfaces. Ornamental lathes were Rube Goldberg-like contraptions that married woodturning and metalworking lathes with the milling machine.

After the initial turning process, an ornamental lathe could turn and mill flutes, spirals, and screw threads, as well as intricate patterns into the work. This was accomplished by applying single-pointed fixed tools in the slides of the machine (like the slides of a metal lathe) and small milling cutters (much akin to a modern router bit) to the work. The spindle could be indexed and could also be slowly advanced by hand on a screw thread. Since ornamental lathes were treadle driven, the work had to be small and of a hard, durable wood such as boxwood, granadilla, and ebony. Ivory and ivory nut (tagua) were also popular ornamental turning materials that remain so today.

Ornamental turning has enjoyed a small but passionate following and experienced a rebirth in the late 20th century. There are two reasonably priced attachments for normal woodturning lathes that bring ornamental turning to the masses. Antique ornamental lathes (built in the 19th century) are hard to find and go for thousands of dollars. Lawler Gear Corp. (see Resources on p. 184) builds a true ornamental turning machine, which goes for about $15,000. I'll look more at ornamental turning in chapter 5.

Setting Up a Lathe

S etting up a lathe involves more than just shoehorning the machine into an available space in the workshop. You need to consider workflow, machine placement, chip removal, ventilation, electrical service, lighting, and tool storage.

Workflow

The lathe should be placed in such a way that work can flow naturally to and from other machines in the shop (see the illustration on p. 36). Billets for spindle turning are often jointed and planed square. They are then cut to length on a table saw or radial-arm saw. Keeping this flow in mind when placing the lathe will save unnecessary trips across the workshop. Access to the bandsaw, which is often used to round up faceplate work before it is mounted in the lathe, may be important depending on your work. And whatever type of turning you do, it's a good idea to mount the grinder and buffer close to the lathe so you won't have far to walk to sharpen your tools.

Machine Placement

Most people tend to put a lathe against a wall, but I think that placing it at right angles or at a 45° angle to a wall makes more sense. You still have the wall for tool racks, but lathe access is much better. And if your lathe has a sheet-metal box-type stand, you need enough room in back of it to

Plan Your Lathe Setup

B efore you install a lathe, taking time to plan things such as its placement, electrical access, and tool storage will save hours, days, and even months in increased production time down the road.

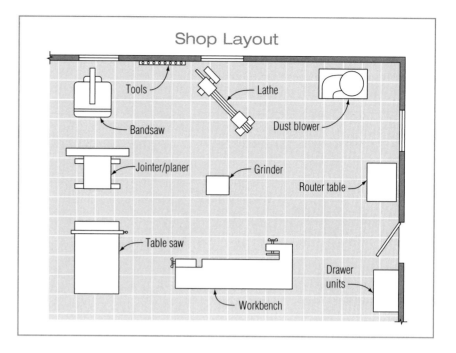

Shop Layout

Tools

Bandsaw

Lathe

Dust blower

Jointer/planer

Grinder

Router table

Table saw

Drawer units

Workbench

sweep, since more than half the chips will accumulate there. Putting a lathe against a wood or metal post is another good option. Electrical outlets, lights, the grinder, and tool racks can be mounted on the post, turning what might otherwise be a dead area into useful space.

Once you've actually positioned your lathe, it needs to be leveled. Test for level parallel to and across the bed ways using a standard builder's level. If you need to level the stand, use wood shims rather than metal because wood is more resilient. A thin sheet of industrial rubber under each leg can help reduce vibration. I've used scrap truck inner tube successfully, cementing the tube to a 3-in. to 4-in. square of ½-in. plywood and placing a square under each corner of the machine. I place additional shims of ⅛-in. Masonite on top of the base plywood shim for fine adjustment.

Now is a good time to consider machine height. A good rule of thumb is to have the spindle centerline at elbow height or just a touch higher. For most people, this height is between 40 in. and 44 in. To raise the height of the lathe, add wood blocks with rubber glued to the underside.

For normal spindle turning, a lathe need not be bolted to the floor. In fact, I prefer the flexibility that leaving it unbolted allows—if my lathe needs to be moved for some reason, it's an easy matter, and I don't have to drill holes in my shop floor. If I have to turn some heavy work that will cause the machine to walk, I weigh down the machine by draping sand bags over the legs or placing them on the box section or shelf below my machine.

Make Your Own Stand

If you are short or tall, making a stand not only saves money but also gives you exactly the right spindle height for your stature.

Chip Removal and Ventilation

A lathe generates such a large amount of dust and chips that it is difficult to extract it all with a dust-collection system. If your shop has a dust-collection system, it's a good idea to locate a pickup port near the lathe. By placing a hose as close as possible to the work, much of the dust from sanding can be vacuumed away. You can also wheel in portable dust blowers and clamp a suitable wood bracket to the lathe to hold the pickup hose close to the work.

Another good idea is to install an air-filtration system above or near your lathe. Such systems are mounted on the ceiling of your shop and have to be sized to the workspace so that all the air in the room changes every few minutes. If properly sized, they dramatically reduce the dust level in the shop.

If you don't have a dust-collection or air-filtration system, being able to open doors and windows will help. In good weather, placing an exhaust fan in the window near your lathe will carry most of the dust outside, which will not only make a turning session more enjoyable but also will be better for your health. For more on dust protection, see "Safety Equipment" on pp. 98–101.

Electrical Service

It's important to have good access to electrical outlets at your lathe. Not only should there be an outlet for the lathe itself but also enough 120-volt outlets for portable power tools that will be used with the lathe, such as electric drills, sanders, and routers. (You'll probably need at least four outlets.) Avoid extension cords because long cords can cause power loss, which will result in lower voltage at the machine and in turn will cause the motor to run hotter. Although this may not be enough to trip the breaker or blow a fuse, it can shorten the life of the motor. You will also notice less power and more frequent stalling of the machine. The cord can also trip you.

Make sure that you have properly grounded outlets that meet your local electrical building codes. Electrical codes vary from region to region, so it's difficult to state what will be acceptable in your locality. Minimum standards for an outlet are that it should be a properly grounded, fused circuit with wire gauge adequate for the required amperage. Some localities may require additional measures, such as running wires in conduit.

If you have an electrician run a new circuit, be sure to install ground-fault circuit interrupter (GFCI) breakers at the same time. GFCI breakers are code in most states for bathrooms, basements, and garages. They sense any problem in grounding and break the circuit, saving countless lives. They are well worth the money. If you find that your lathe is continually tripping the GFCI breaker, there's a problem with your lathe. Get it fixed!

If possible, run your lathe on 220-volt rather than 110-volt current. Your motor will start more quickly and overcome turning resistance more easily. It will also be slightly cheaper to operate the motor on the higher voltage. While it is tempting to put a 10-ft. or 15-ft. lead on your motor, it's not a good idea. The plug at the end of the cord provides a second disconnect should the switch fail or if it is unsafe to get to the switch. Also it is imperative to unplug the machine during certain operations such as maintenance. Although local codes vary from state to state, they often specify that this plug/disconnect should be a short distance from the machine. OSHA code, if applicable, is even more stringent.

Lighting

The importance of good lighting at the lathe cannot be overemphasized. I prefer to work by natural light, so the lathes I work on most often are near windows. Natural light is especially helpful when matching stains and colors. Fluorescent lighting tends to be very cold, so I opt for full-spectrum tubes that more closely mimic sunlight.

Although good general lighting is all that is necessary, it may also be useful to attach a work lamp to the lathe. Sophisticated models with long articulated arms are available at discount stores. Such a light will be helpful for fine detail work or for seeing inside hollow work such as bowls.

Tool Storage

Tool storage around a lathe can present a real problem. Shelves or drawers under the lathe fill with chips. Tool racks attached to the front of the lathe tend to get in the way. Without a tool rack of some sort, you'll end up balancing three tools on the bed and one will invariably fall off, point first. After I'd made hundreds of trips to the grinder to fix such mishaps, master woodturner Palmer Sharpless showed me a simple rack that fits between the bed ways. It supports a working complement of three to five tools and can be moved anywhere along the bed with the needs of the job (see the illustration above).

For the rest of your tools, there are several options. One of my favorites is to mount a tool rack on the wall or post near your lathe. A serviceable rack can be made quickly by drilling holes of the appropriate diameter in a strip of wood, then affixing it to the wall. Design it with minimal horizontal surfaces to collect dust.

Palmer Sharpless's Tool Rack

Cleat fits between bed ways and supports center rack on lathe bed.

12 in.

8 in.

Hire an Electrician

If you're at all uncertain about electrical matters, hire a competent licensed electrician to do any wiring you need in your shop.

Holding the Work

Now that you have your lathe set up and running, it's time to think about turning something. But first you need a way to hold the work in the lathe. I've always maintained that I can turn anything, if given a way to mount it in my lathe. This is where chucking comes in. Technically, a chuck is any device that holds work in the lathe. It can be a set of centers, a faceplate, an elaborately manufactured jaw-type chuck, or a simple shopmade glue block.

Understanding the difference between spindle turning and faceplate turning is central to the concept of chucking. In spindle turning, the grain of the wood being turned runs between the centers of the lathe, that is, parallel to the axis of the lathe. In faceplate turning, the grain of the work runs at right angles to the axis of the lathe (see the illustration on p. 5). Although turning between centers is commonly associated with spindle turning, it's possible to hold work this way and yet be faceplate turning. Similarly, it's possible to have something screwed onto a faceplate and still be spindle turning. The screws in this case would be into the end grain of the wood. Remember that the orientation of the grain, not how the work is held, dictates the type of turning. Each type of work also requires different tools and turning techniques, as I will discuss in this chapters 6 and 8.

Centers

The oldest and simplest way to hold work in the lathe is between a set of centers, one mounted in the headstock and the other in the tailstock. Most spindle work is held this way. Centers are a fast and reliable way to mount work, and they allow unlimited chucking and unchucking, which is an advantage when you want to trial-fit turned furniture parts or to allow stains and finishes to dry between lathe operations.

DRIVE CENTERS

The drive center, or spur center, mounts in the headstock spindle. It both holds the work and transmits power to it. Except on very inexpensive lathes (where the center screws on the headstock spindle), the shank of the center is a Morse taper that fits into a matching socket in the spindle. The business end of the center is a small central point surrounded by spurs

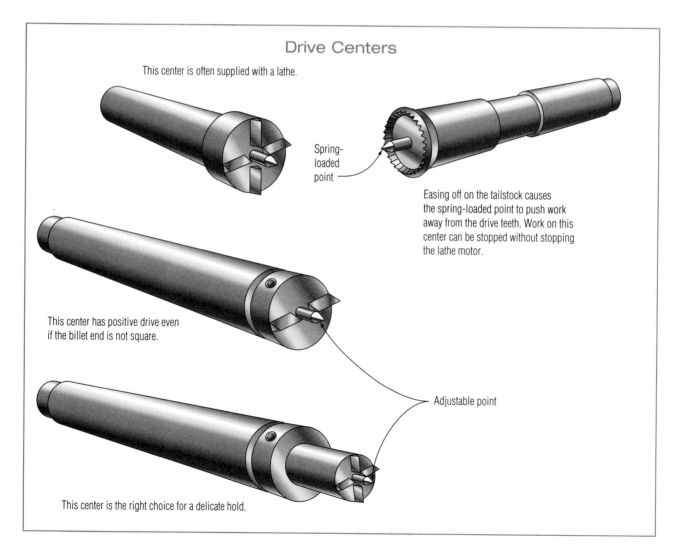

Drive Centers

This center is often supplied with a lathe.

Spring-loaded point

Easing off on the tailstock causes the spring-loaded point to push work away from the drive teeth. Work on this center can be stopped without stopping the lathe motor.

This center has positive drive even if the billet end is not square.

Adjustable point

This center is the right choice for a delicate hold.

If the billet end is not square, a four-spur drive center drives on only one tine and the work constantly walks off-center. A two-spur center can be turned to drive on both tines, eliminating the problem.

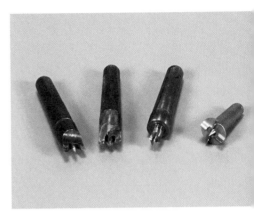

A two-spur center (far left) drives just as well as a four-spur model (second from left). A mini center (second from right) is necessary when a delicate footprint is desired, such as when turning very small spindles, pen blanks, and the like. The center at far right is typical of those supplied with economy lathes; it is built on a short Morse taper.

(also called tines). The central point should protrude $\frac{1}{16}$ in. to $\frac{1}{8}$ in. beyond the face of the tines to ensure centering of the work before the tines bite in. On better drive centers, the central point is removable and adjustable for the amount it stands proud of the tines.

Drive centers are sold in two-spur and four-spur models. A two-spur center is generally better because it drives as well as a four-spur one and can be oriented to give positive drive no matter what the contour of the end of the turning billet (see the illustration on the facing page). If the surface is irregular, a four-spur center will drive on only one tine, which can cause the work to go off-center and even kick out of the lathe in extreme cases. If your lathe comes with a four-spur center, you can easily modify it by grinding away two of the tines. Mini centers are also available, which are used where a small footprint is desired, as in the turning of a knob. The diameter of the tines is so small that minis are much less sensitive about how square the end of a billet is.

Each tine of a spur center comes to a chisel edge. These edges must not be in line with each other or the center will become a wedge and split the work. If the tines become dull or damaged, you can grind them back to a chisel edge, making sure you grind on the bevel side only. You should also keep the central point sharp. If it is removable, it's easy to sharpen it by mounting it in a cordless drill and simply touching it to a running grinder.

It's normally not necessary to pound the center into the work or to saw lines in the end of the billet, as some turners recommend, to achieve positive drive. Pressure from the tailstock is generally sufficient to drive

Steb centers are great for furniture work where the ends are cut square because they allow you to stop the work without stopping the lathe simply by easing the tailstock pressure.

Place the center-punched end of the billet on the center pin of the steb center, and catch the other center-punch mark with the tailstock center. Once you tighten the tailstock, the work is securely held.

To inspect your work, simply loosen the tailstock a bit and place your open hand against the spinning billet. It will stop instantly. To continue with your work, tighten the tailstock again.

the tines into the work. Even on small lathes, there is tremendous mechanical advantage in the screw-thread mechanism of the tailstock handwheel.

It's a good idea to grind a nick on the outer radial surface of one of the tines. Whenever you remove work from the lathe but plan to rechuck it, make a pencil mark on the workpiece next to the nick so you can reposition it accurately. With wear, sharpening, and mishaps such as drops on concrete, each tine gets to be a different length. Unless the work is repositioned on the drive center exactly the way it was removed, perfect centering will be difficult. Your pencil mark and nick make rechucking simple.

Standard drive centers are available in Morse-taper sizes #1, #2, and #3. If you plan to turn miniature work such as dollhouse furniture, a standard drive center is too large and will get in the way. The solution is to buy a mini drive center, which has a smaller outside diameter ranging from ⅜ in. to ½ in.

Lately my preference in drive centers for turning furniture parts has become steb centers, which feature a serrated ring with a spring-loaded central point. I center-punch each end of my billets and place the mark on the center point of the steb center with the lathe running. I catch the punch mark at the other end of the billet with the tailstock center and advance the tailstock so that the work catches securely and turning progresses normally (see the top photo at right on the facing page). The great advantage is that I don't have to shut off the lathe to check my work. I just loosen the tailstock a tad and the center point pushes the work off the serrated ring. I touch the work lightly and it stops dead (see the bottom photo on the facing page). After inspection I simply tighten the tailstock and instantly start turning again. It is easy and much quicker than stopping and starting the motor.

Steb centers come in 1-in. and ½-in. sizes, which are measured by the diameter of the serrated ring. I would not work without either. The 1-in. steb center handles normal-sized furniture parts well, while the ½-in. size is perfect for knobs and other small items. A steb center only works well on prepared billets (with square ends) of reasonable size; a 3-in. square table leg is about the biggest it can handle. If work is taken off of the lathe, rechucking is much easier with a steb center because it tends to center more accurately than a normal drive center.

TAILSTOCK CENTERS

The tailstock center, which mounts in the tailstock spindle, centers the work and exerts force through itself to the drive center in the headstock. It also gives radial support to the work, thereby holding it in the lathe. As with drive centers, the tailstock center has a Morse-taper shaft, but the business end is quite different.

There are two types of tailstock centers: dead centers and live centers (see the illustration on p. 44). The simplest dead center is a 60° point, but the more traditional design—a cup center—consists of a simple pivot bearing surrounded by a raised ring. Because the center is stationary, it needs to be lubricated to reduce friction and heat buildup from the rotating workpiece. Any grease will do as a lubricant—I once used butter from a high school cafeteria to get me through a demonstration. No matter what the lubricant, you can expect some burning with a dead center. The benefit of a cup center is that the ring around the point retains grease, so lubrication is better and makes the work less prone to splitting.

There is one advantage to using a dead center: You can touch it with a tool (lightly) and it will not dull the edge as a live center will. Occasionally a turning situation, such as when you have to turn around the end of the billet right up to the center, makes a 60° dead center worth using. Dead centers are inexpensive, and lathes have traditionally come with a dead center in the accessory kit.

Live centers are a great improvement over dead centers because the center point is mounted on a ball bearing and rotates with the spinning work, eliminating the need for lubrication and the risk of burning. In addition, you can exert much greater force on the work with a live center, which means that the work is held more securely. Because of these overwhelming advantages, even entry-level lathes generally come with a live center in the accessory kit these days. Unfortunately, it's typically not a very good live center—in fact, you often would be better off with a dead one.

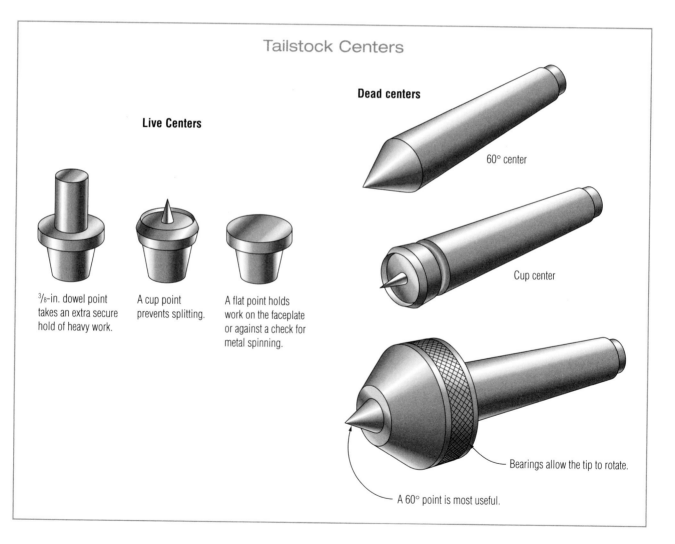

Tailstock Centers

Live Centers

Dead centers

60° center

Cup center

³/₈-in. dowel point takes an extra secure hold of heavy work.

A cup point prevents splitting.

A flat point holds work on the faceplate or against a check for metal spinning.

Bearings allow the tip to rotate.

A 60° point is most useful.

At far left is a typical economy live center supplied with many lathes. The next four are full-featured live centers with four points (left to right): a cup; an extended cup; a core center, which can be driven into a ½-in. hole on very long and heavy work; and a 60-degree point mounted in the center. Second from right is a heavy-duty center by Oneway, which is a normal cup point as shown, but by attaching the cone at the far right it will center large bores or, when reversed, go over squares, hexes, and such.

Better live centers are sold with two or three interchangeable points. The 60° point and cup center are standard designs, and some live centers also come with a third flat-faced insert (see the photo above), which is used for special tasks such as holding a bowl in a jam chuck or spinning metal.

The idea behind the cup center is that the outside ring prevents the work from splitting. In my experience, a 60° point has no greater tendency to split work than a cup point. What's more, it holds in a much smaller area, which allows you to turn nearly the center of the billet, and wears much better in service. For these reasons, the 60° point is the only point I give my students. You can often get 60° live centers from metalworking-supply houses at bargain prices. Even though these centers are designed for metalworking lathes, they work fine for woodturning. The one time a cup point center is necessary is when chucking split turnings. Split turnings have a paper joint in the middle and would be split prematurely by a 60° center.

Faceplates are offered in a wide variety of sizes and qualities.

Faceplates

Faceplates are used to hold work that can't be supported (or that you don't want to be supported) by a tailstock. Since this situation encompasses most faceplate work, the type of turning has been named for the chucking method. As mentioned previously, however, it's the orientation of the grain that makes it facework, not how the work is held.

A faceplate is simply a metal disk with a threaded hub that screws onto the headstock spindle. Circles of holes around the periphery allow work to be fastened to the plate with screws. Most faceplates have a flat surface, but the better models have a ledge around the outer edge that allows the plate to better seat flat on uneven surfaces. Today, many face-

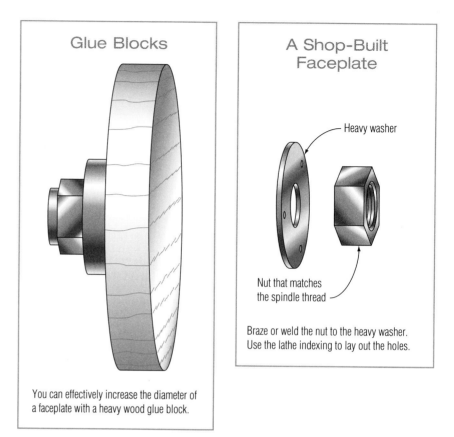

Glue Blocks

You can effectively increase the diameter of a faceplate with a heavy wood glue block.

A Shop-Built Faceplate

Heavy washer

Nut that matches the spindle thread

Braze or weld the nut to the heavy washer. Use the lathe indexing to lay out the holes.

plates are made from cast aluminum, which works fine for most operations but is not suitable for large-diameter and heavy work. For heavy-duty faceplate turning, there is no substitute for cast iron or steel.

Faceplates are available in various diameters depending on the lathe manufacturer, but the most common sizes are 3 in., 6 in., and 9 in. Most woodworkers think that they need a large faceplate, but for the vast majority of your work, a 3-in. plate (often known as a "bowl chuck") will serve you much better. Because the base of a knob or a bowl should be about one-third its widest dimension, it would be next to impossible to turn the base on a 6-in. faceplate, unless the work is more than 18 in. dia.

Most bowl chucks have only three holes around the circumference. It's a good idea to drill and countersink an extra hole between each of the originals for a total of six. This allows you to use six screws in demanding situations, thereby greatly increasing the holding power of the faceplate. I recommend that you buy four or five 3-in. faceplates so you don't have to mount and unmount them all the time. You'll need a larger faceplate only if you plan to turn large-diameter, heavy work, and even then you can usually get away with attaching a large glue block to a smaller faceplate (see the illustration above left).

Faceplates are manufactured to fit standard spindle sizes (see the chart on p. 13). If you have a lathe with an oddball spindle size, you can make your own faceplate, provided you can find a nut that fits the spindle. Have an industrial weld shop weld a large, heavy, flat washer to the nut (see the illustration at right on the facing page). Drill and countersink evenly spaced screw holes around the periphery of the washer. You can use the lathe's indexing mechanism (see pp. 18–19) to lay out the holes.

Work flying off of faceplates presents the greatest safety hazard in turning, so it is imperative to ensure that your work is securely attached to the faceplate and the lathe is set to a low speed before you begin turning.

SCREWS

In the past, wood screws were used to attach work to a faceplate, but today's sheet-metal screws provide a much surer hold. Sheet-metal screws have a straight body and 45° thread profile that bites into wood much better than wood screws (see the illustration below). They are also mildly heat treated, which gives them added strength and toughness.

As a minimum, you should use #10 sheet-metal screws to secure work to the faceplate. I use two sizes: #12 x 1 in. for the lion's share of my work and #12 x 1½ in. when extra surety is needed. Under no circumstances should you use drywall screws—they're hard and brittle and might snap under load.

Sheet-metal screws are available in slotted, Phillips, hex, and Robertson head design. Robertson, or square-drive, screws require a special screw-

<table>
<tr><td>**The Right Screw**</td></tr>
</table>

The best screw for holding work on a faceplate is a #10 or larger hex-head sheet-metal screw.

A fast and reliable way to secure a faceplate to a workpiece is to use hex-head sheet-metal screws and a speeder (left). If the screws come loose once the work is mounted on the lathe, they can be tightened with a box wrench (right).

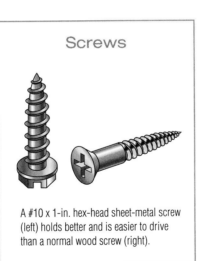

Screws

A #10 x 1-in. hex-head sheet-metal screw (left) holds better and is easier to drive than a normal wood screw (right).

driver, but they lend themselves well to using cordless electric drills for taking the drudgery out of screwing work to plates. The only problem with the electric drill is that it's easy to overtighten and strip the thread.

I prefer to use hex-head sheet-metal screws and a speeder, which is a cranklike automotive tool for turning bolts quickly (see the photo on p. 47). A speeder takes ⅜-in. sockets directly and works much like a bit brace. It allows quick, positive, and painless turning of the screws without the risk of stripping them. And because I'm the power behind the speeder, I know the battery in my speeder is always charged.

Another advantage of hex-head screws is that they can be easily tightened with a small box wrench once the faceplate is mounted on the headstock spindle. It's not unusual for one or more of the faceplate screws to come loose while the lathe is running, and with other screw designs you have to unscrew the faceplate from the spindle to tighten them.

GLUE BLOCKS

For faceplate work such as a stool top, the work is often simply screwed directly to the faceplate. Because the screw holes are on the bottom of the stool, they will be seen only by the snoopy. The trend today, however, is to leave no trace of chucking. One way to avoid screw holes in the work when using a faceplate is to leave extra stock at the base of the piece and then cut above the screws. A much less wasteful way to avoid screw holes is to use a glue block.

To make a glue block, bandsaw a hardwood block to a diameter slightly larger than the faceplate. The block should be thick enough to

When the face is dead flat with a straight edge, it is square to the headstock spindle.

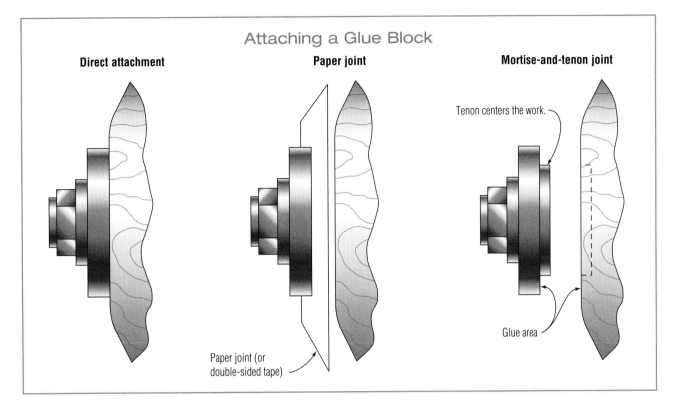

Attaching a Glue Block

Direct attachment

Paper joint

Mortise-and-tenon joint

Tenon centers the work.

Paper joint (or double-sided tape)

Glue area

more than bury the screws. (I use 5/4 material because it's thick enough to get a cutoff tool between the screws and the work.) Mount the block on a faceplate, and scrape it flat with a large dome scraper. Check with a straightedge to make sure the face is flat.

While it is tempting to simply joint one face flat and then thickness-plane to the appropriate thickness before bandsawing rounds, this scheme does not work out well in practice. There is enough variation in thickness from the average thickness planer to impart considerable runout to the work once the glue block is attached. On the other hand, scraping the glue block flat in the lathe creates a face that is flat and square to the axis of rotation. This makes a big difference in the amount of runout at the periphery when mounting a 12-in. or 14-in. stool seat or a platter.

In light of the above, I simply bandsaw rounds from reasonably flat roughsawn planks and screw directly to the roughsawn material. As long as the screws are well tightened, the roughsawn surface is fine.

It is best to drill pilot holes in glue blocks before mounting to avoid split-ting. There are three ways to attach the glue block to the work: direct gluing, a paper joint, or a mortise-and-tenon joint (see the illustration above).

Direct attachment With this method, the glue block and attached face-plate are simply glued to the center of the work. This method works best when you need extreme strength in chucking in the hold, for example, when the piece is heavy or large or when building special jigs and fixtures.

It is imperative to use a good-quality glue and to achieve a joinery-level fit between the work and glue block.

Once you have scraped the glue block flat (as well as square to the axis of rotation), you need only get one surface of the work flat because you will make the face flat and square to the axis of rotation during the turning process. The surface to be flattened may be jointed already; if not, you can flatten it with a handplane. Once the surface is prepared, attach the work to the block by using plenty of glue and clamping the joint. Be sure to allow sufficient time for the glue to thoroughly cure before turning. Your lathe itself is generally the best clamp and gives you exact centering in the process.

For trays, stools, and the like, I lay out the desired circle with trammels on the face side of the work (the side away from the chuck), then bandsaw to the trammel line and apply glue to the glue block. There is a small dimple where the trammel centered. Pick up this dimple with your live center, and use the pressure of the tailstock ram to force the work against the glue block on the exact center.

If you are mounting to green wood (as bowl turners often do), you will need to use cyanoacrylate glue because other glues will not hold to the moist surface. Called Super Glue, cyanoacrylate glue can be found at model shops and good woodworking-supply houses.

Once the work is mounted in the lathe, test the joint with a good two-handed tug. After you've finished turning the work, simply cut off slightly to the glue block side of the joint. You can now handplane or orbital-sand the last traces of the glue block away from the work.

Finding Kraft Paper

The best source of brown kraft paper is a used grocery shopping bag.

Your lathe itself is the best bar clamp you can find for glue-ups.

MANY TURNERS TODAY use double-sided tape in place of a paper joint. While double-sided tape works out well for chucking, it is not effective for split turnings. There are also some safety considerations when using double-sided tape. First, it is imperative that a cloth-based tape be used. Most of the "carpet tape" at local hardware stores is foam based, which does not have sufficient strength. Fabric-based tape is available through industrial distribution chains.

The second consideration is that sufficient pressure must be applied to the tape joint to achieve adequate adhesion. The joint should either be clamped or pressed in a vise. Often the tailstock ram may be used to apply sufficient pressure. Clamping for a few seconds ensures good adhesion.

Many people tape directly to a faceplate, which works fine with standard Delta-style flat-faced plates. My preference for faceplates with a raised lip at the edge renders them unsuitable for tape. I can overcome this by attaching a glue block.

The other considerations of the tape joint are identical to those of the paper joint. I do not like to tape as well as glue and paper, however. With glue you have a bit of open time to slide things around into perfect position, but with tape you get only one shot. Releasing the taped work from the chuck can also be problematic. I have broken or pulled wood grain from the work when breaking tape joints. If the joint proves very stubborn, soak the edges of the joint for 15 to 20 minutes with xylo to break down the adhesive.

Paper-joint chucking In paper-joint chucking, a piece of brown kraft paper is juxtaposed between the glue block and the work. The work is easy to remove from the glue block after chucking because the joint will separate along the paper joint. A joinery-level fit is still required. Although I prefer to use hide glue, yellow or white glue works just as well. Other than the paper, the joint is handled like any other woodworking joint: Apply plenty of glue on both sides of the paper, and clamp for the manufacturer's recommended clamping time. As in direct attachment, your lathe is the best clamp to apply pressure at the exact center and to achieve perfect centering.

To break the joint when you're done, give it a good rap at the periphery, but hit at the end grain, not the face grain, side because there is more strength in that orientation. If the separation proves cantankerous, place a sharp chisel in the glueline (again at the long grain edge), and give it a sharp rap with a mallet.

Paper joints have excellent sheer strength (they resist the rotating forces of the lathe) but poor axial strength. Therefore, I always keep a tailstock against the work for as long as possible. This gets you through the roughing process without putting substantial force on the paper joint. Paper joints need to have a reasonable area in proportion to the diameter of the work. A good starting point is one-third the diameter of the workpiece, so a 12-in. platter would require a 4-in.-dia. glue block. But much depends on the skill of the turner. The beginner who catches now and then will need the paper joint to cover plenty of area, while the seasoned old hand can get away with much less.

Mortise-and-tenon joints Bowl turners most often use this method of glue-block chucking. It is particularly useful when something on a face-plate (or screw chuck) needs to be turned around for further turning, such as a bowl. To use this method, scrape a shallow mortise in the base of the bowl just before removing it from the faceplate or screw chuck. Next, mount the glue block on a faceplate or screw chuck and scrape it flat, then scrape a tenon on the glue block to match the mortise. It does not have to be a press fit ($\frac{1}{64}$ in. to $\frac{1}{32}$ in. of slop is actually best), and the tenon should not bottom out in the mortise (see the illustration below).

Apply glue only to the shoulder area, mate the two pieces, and apply pressure with the tailstock ram. Cyanoacrylate glue works well and is necessary if you're turning green wood. I generally apply the glue to the glue block and spray the catalyst on the piece. When the two mate, the glue dries within 30 seconds, so you have to have everything right.

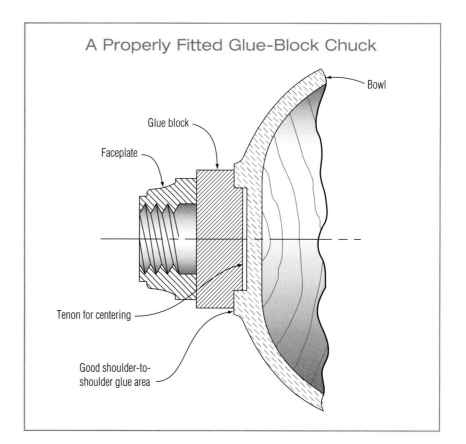

A Properly Fitted Glue-Block Chuck

Bowl

Glue block

Faceplate

Tenon for centering

Good shoulder-to-shoulder glue area

Chuck manufacturers offer a wide variety of jaws. Left to right: Nova lever with standard jaws; Nova lever with heavy stepped jaws that hold internally at two diameters; Nova lever with finger jaws especially suited for holding dowels, knobs, and such; Oneway lever with large-diameter, low-profile jaws suitable for internal and external holds on large, heavy faceplate work; and Oneway lever with rubber baby bumper jaws holding a bowl for reverse turning.

These antique smoking-pipe chucks are a cross between jam chucks and collet chucks. A wood ring slips over the chuck to force the collet closed around the work. There are also chucks to mount a sawblade (left) and a grinding wheel (right) in the lathe.

Special-Purpose Chucks

Centers and faceplates are the two basic ways of holding work on the lathe. They'll cope with the majority of your turning requirements; indeed, you could turn for a lifetime using nothing more. There are times, however, when other chucking methods can make life easier. Special-purpose chucks can be invaluable for grabbing odd-shaped work, small work, and finished work that requires modification. In production work, a special-purpose chuck can often speed things up considerably. Let's look at the vast array of special-purpose chucks that you can buy or make yourself.

<table>
<tr><td>Choosing Jaws</td></tr>
<tr><td>Some manufacturers have jaws for highly specialized purposes. When shopping for a chuck, it is good to see how the jaws offered by a prospective manufacturer fit in with what you plan to turn.</td></tr>
</table>

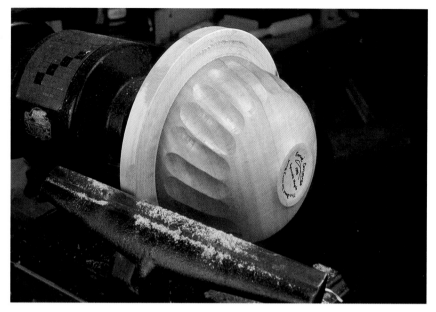

Jam chucks are used primarily to hold small items in the lathe, but bowls can also be jam-chucked to allow turning of the base.

With this information, you'll be able to tackle any turning job safely and confidently.

JAM CHUCKS

One of the simplest and oldest homemade chucks is the jam, or cup, chuck. It's a sure, simple way to grab small items without leaving marks in the work. I use it to hold anything from knobs and finials to trays and bowls. Until the early 20th century, a turner would typically have a range of jam chucks made from gun metal by a local machinist. They worked splendidly.

The body of a jam chuck should be spindle-turned from a 3-in.-dia. to 4-in.-dia. piece of close-grained hardwood. Maple, ash, and beech all work very well. Since scrap stock of this diameter is hard to come by, I normally glue two pieces of 8/4 stock together. Yellow glue works fine, but be sure to plane both surfaces for a perfect joint, use plenty of glue, and clamp for a full 24 hours.

In the old days, a tap hole was drilled through the center of the billet, and it was threaded to screw directly onto the headstock spindle (see the bottom photo on p. 53). Since suitable wood taps are unavailable today and wood threads do not work out well in end grain anyway, it's easier to screw the billet to a faceplate. (Remember I suggested buying extra faceplates?) Attach a 3-in. to 5-in. section of the billet to the faceplate with 1-in. or 1½-in. sheet-metal screws.

As shown in the photos on pp. 56–57, mount the faceplate in your lathe, and true up the outside diameter of the billet with a roughing-out

Start Small

The first law of jam chucking is never to chuck something you are not prepared to be hit in the head with. For that reason, it's a good idea to start with small items.

gouge. Face the end, and drill a ⅜-in. hole through the center with a drill bit mounted in the tailstock. The drill hole allows you to use a knockout bar to eject the work from the chuck.

Next, scrape a tapered pocket into the face of the chuck that is the diameter of the work you want to hold. The taper should be about 3° inclusive (the same angle as a Morse taper). To cut the taper, I use a special scraper that can easily be ground from an old file and a long-forgotten auxiliary tool rest, called an arm rest (for more about scrapers and the arm rest, see pp. 137 and 77, respectively). You'll quickly find the right taper— if it's too steep or not steep enough, the chuck won't hold the work.

Most work for jam-chucking is turned between centers or on a faceplate before it's mounted in the jam chuck. Remember to square the end of the work face that will go into the jam chuck. Insert the work into the chuck by lining it up as square as possible and giving it a solid rap with a hammer. Next, turn the lathe over by hand, watching for eccentricity. Rap the edge opposite the point that is most eccentric and retest, then continue until the work is perfectly centered. Rubbing some blackboard chalk on the walls of the pocket will add greatly to the chuck's holding power.

To use a jam chuck, you have to be able to turn well enough so that a catch is the exception rather than the rule because a catch can throw the work from the chuck's embrace—or at least throw it out of kilter. Jam-chucking is a skill, so the first few times will be an uphill battle; once learned it will become second nature. Your first jam-chucking is best done on small items, such as the box shown in the photo essay on pp. 56–57.

I've successfully chucked items as big as boccie balls, and I jam-chuck bowls regularly. If I have the least doubt about using a jam chuck, however, I add security by trapping the work in the chuck with a tailstock. I also keep speeds moderate, often no more than 200 rpm to 300 rpm for bowls. (This is another reason I find variable speed indispensable.)

COLLET CHUCKS

A slightly different version of the jam chuck is to turn it into a collet chuck. To make this chuck, mount a piece of wood on a faceplate with sheet-metal screws. (Be sure to screw into end grain so that the wood is aligned in spindle-turning orientation.) Drill a hole in the very center that is the diameter of the tenon on the knob (or finial) you are going to hold. Next, turn a gentle taper on the outside of the chuck, and split it into fours with a backsaw or bandsaw. Pound a wood or metal ring onto the taper to force the collet closed. (Don't be tempted to use automotive hose clamps—they don't have the closing power for this task.)

Often a metal ring of suitable size can be found, but it is little trouble to turn a wood one. It's best to faceplate-turn the ring, but remember to keep the cross section robust for strength. I like to make the chuck a bit long for several reasons. First, it can be split far enough back to give the jaws plenty of spring. Second, it may be cut back if you hit it with a tool

Making and Using a Jam Chuck

1 Attach a faceplate to the end of the chuck blank and mount it in the lathe. This is spindle turning, so we are screwing into end grain.

2 True up the body of the chuck and square (face) the end. Here I am using a spindle gouge to face the billet, but a big scraper and the arm rest work great for this task as well.

3 Drill a hole ¹⁄₁₆ in. bigger than the diameter of your knockout bar through the center of the chuck. Most knockout bars are ³⁄₈ in. dia., so ⁷⁄₁₆ in. works well. A spindle gouge actually makes a good drill if presented with the point at dead center and the flute turned about 45° to the left (facing 10 o'clock).

4 Scrape a tapered pocket into the face of the chuck that is the same diameter as the work to be held.

5 Tap the work into the pocket, and true up as necessary. A carpenter's hammer is the perfect tool.

6 You're now free to work on the piece. Here, I use a spindle gouge to turn the outside of the box.

or for subsequent jobs. By tapping the ring in place to where the jaws are held but not compressed, it may be drilled out to larger diameters.

TAPERED MANDRELS

Tapered mandrels, or cone chucks, are essentially jam chucks turned inside out. They're a good way to hold small items such as napkin rings (or the closing ring for a collet chuck) and a great way to hold hollow spindle turnings between centers. The advantages of tapered mandrels are that the

This homemade chuck is no more than a shop-built collet chuck. The outside of the chuck is turned to a gentle taper, and the tip is partially split by bandsawing or backsawing. A ring of suitable diameter is then added. By forcing the ring down over the taper, the chuck is closed.

You can turn small items like the closing ring for a collet chuck on a tapered mandrel.

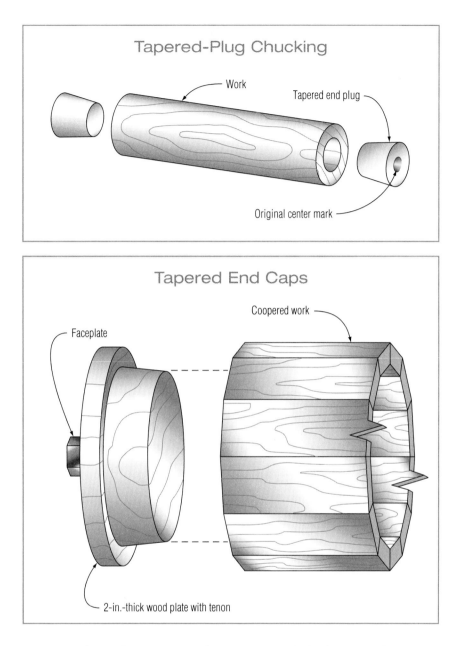

Tapered-Plug Chucking

Work

Tapered end plug

Original center mark

Tapered End Caps

Coopered work

Faceplate

2-in.-thick wood plate with tenon

outside of the work can be turned concentric with the bore and that the work can be chucked and unchucked quickly and held safely.

To mount an item such as a closing ring for a collet chuck, start with a billet of wood on a faceplate, just as if making a jam chuck. However, to make a tapered mandrel, turn the outside to a gentle 3° taper. Place the bored-out ring over the mandrel, and using a block of wood and a hammer, alternately "adjust" until it runs true. You can now finish-turn and sand the outer surfaces of the ring.

As in the case of this coopered birdhouse, the headstock mandrel can be left on the screw chuck.

Depending on the size of the central hole, you can mount hollow spindle turnings on the lathe with tapered plugs or tapered end caps. Tapered plugs are used for cylindrical objects (such as a pepper mill) with a fairly small central bore—anything up to about 1 in. inside diameter (see the top illustration on p. 59). Turn the plugs as a single piece between centers, then saw them apart. Tap the plugs into the ends of the turning, and remount on the lathe on the original center marks. The outside of the object can now be turned concentric with the bore.

Tapered end caps are used with hollow work that has a large central bore (see the bottom illustration on p. 59). This is often coopered work (glued up out of staves), such as birdhouses, buckets, and columns. An important difference from tapered plugs is that the mandrel for each end is faceplate-turned as a separate item. A good way to hold each end cap is to use a large screw chuck, which allows the tapered step in the mandrel to be turned concentric with a center hole. Leave the headstock mandrel on the screw chuck, then insert the tailstock mandrel into the work. The center hole left by the screw chuck is caught by a 60° live center. The work is now safely trapped between centers on the set of mandrels and can be turned easily. I've chucked 12-in.-dia. by 8-ft.-long coopered columns using this method.

PRESSURE-TURNING CHUCKS

A pressure-turning chuck is great for high-production turning, and it is a dandy way to chuck lightweight, flat, round items such as plates. This improvised chuck may also be used to hold work while scraping a dovetail recess for expanding scroll chucks (see p. 73).

The basis of a pressure-turning chuck is a glue block that has been scraped flat, as described previously. Using a drill chuck in the tailstock, drill a pilot hole slightly smaller than a 10d nail three-quarters of the way through the center of the glue block. Pound a 10d nail into the hole so that it bottoms out, then cut off the nail about $\frac{1}{16}$ in. proud of the face of the block and file it to a point (see the top photo below). The easy way to point the nail is by touching a file to the nail with the lathe running.

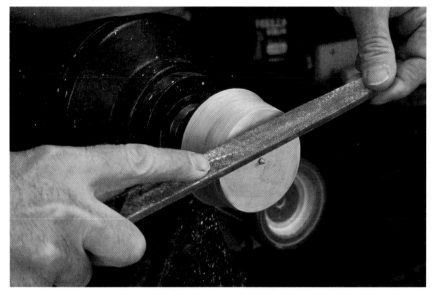

To prepare for pressure turning, file the nail protruding from the glue block to a point.

Both sides of the work can be turned in their entirety, except for the small nub under the tailstock center.

Mount work for pressure turning between the nail block and a live center in the tailstock.

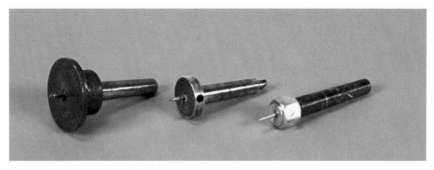

Traditionally, screw chucks were used for light work and were built on Morse-taper blanks.

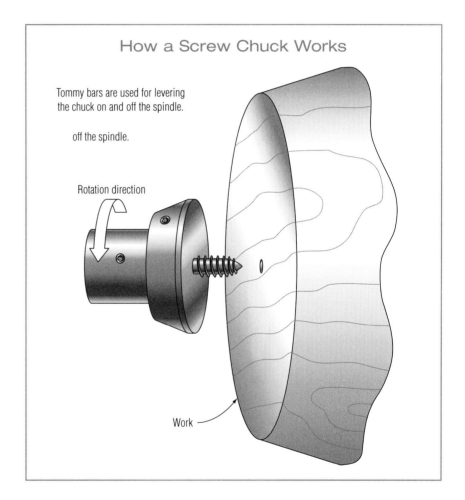

How a Screw Chuck Works

Tommy bars are used for levering the chuck on and off the spindle.

off the spindle.

Rotation direction

Work

Because rounds are laid out with a compass, there will be a center mark on the workpiece. Align this mark on the nail point, and force the work against the glue block with the tailstock spindle (see the photo below right on p. 61). You can do this either by using a flat live-center point in the tailstock or by interposing a small block of wood between a cup center or 60° point and the work. Gluing 180-grit sandpaper to the face of the glue block will provide more positive drive to the work.

Using a pressure-turning chuck, you can completely turn flat work on both sides, except for a small nub under the center point (see the bottom left photo on p. 61). Once the piece is removed from the lathe, you can chisel away this nub and sand it smooth. The only sign of chucking will be a small indent at the center of the plate base.

SCREW CHUCKS

A screw chuck has traditionally been a favorite for holding small items, although it can also hold work as large as a dinner plate. The time-honored design is simplicity itself. A wood screw protrudes from the face of a Morse-taper blank. A small hole, the body diameter of the screw, is drilled in the work to facilitate threading it onto the chuck (see the illus-

The scroll chuck shown on the left is a Oneway chuck, which has a screw included that turns it into a screw chuck. The two center screw chucks are by Jerry Glaser. On the right is a Nova lever scroll chuck with an included screw.

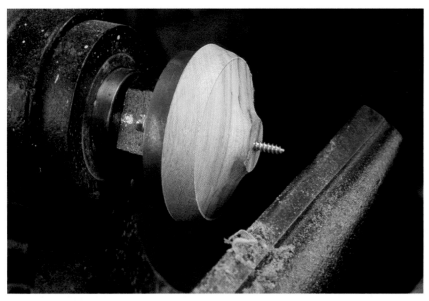

Shop-built screw chucks are an ideal way to hold small work in the lathe, and they make duplication easy.

Lightly touching the point of a skew to the center of the glue block before drilling will ensure that the drill starts perfectly on-center.

tration on p. 62). Since a right-hand thread opposes the rotation direction of the lathe, the work self-tightens on the chuck. You can chuck and un-chuck work from a screw chuck with fair consistency. Screw chucks built on Morse tapers are perfect for turning repetitive parts such as chess pieces and drawer pulls. The small screw leaves little visible evidence of turning (and the screw hole is typically concealed on the finished piece anyway).

Recently, a second type of screw chuck has gained popularity. It has a much bigger screw and is built on a faceplate-like body, which allows it to be threaded onto the headstock spindle (see the top photo on p. 63). The heavy screw has a straight body with a very coarse 45° thread profile. The thread looks much like that on a drywall screw and makes for a very posi-tive hold in wood. Depending on the chuck, a ⅜-in. to ⁷⁄₁₆-in. hole is required for mounting. The more positive drive of the threaded faceplate-like mount, combined with a heavy screw, makes it possible to hold very large work such as bowl blanks. These chucks are also good for furniture bases, trays, and plates.

In recent years, I have come to use heavy screw chucks a great deal. I look at them as a great chucking bargain for the faceplate (especially bowls) turner because one screw chuck will replace a bunch of faceplates. I can mount a heavy bowl blank on a screw chuck and turn the outside, then I can mount a glue block on the same screw and glue the base of the bowl to the glue block to turn the inside of the bowl. Finally, I can mount a disk of plywood on the screw chuck and scrape a groove the diameter of the rim for reverse chucking to turn the base of the bowl (see *Turn a Bowl with Ernie Conover*, The Taunton Press).

When I was a boy, I always made my own screw chucks at the lathe. I still think a shopmade chuck is superior to commercial models for holding small items such as knobs, finials, and chess pieces. The great advantage of a shop-built screw chuck is that you can turn the face of the chuck to the base diameter of the workpiece, which makes duplication of additional pieces easy. Also, you can match the screw in the chuck to the screw that will install the finished turning, as in the case of knobs.

To make a screw chuck, start with a 1-in.- to 1¼-in.-thick glue block, and scrape the face of the glue block to the base diameter of the workpiece. Lightly touch the point of a skew to the center of the glue block, then drill a small hole for the screw in the center of the block with a drill bit secured in a chuck in the tailstock (see the photo on the facing page). Remove the faceplate from the headstock, and screw a suitable wood or sheet-metal screw into the hole in the back of the glue block. Applying some epoxy or cyanoacrylate glue to the screw thread will prevent it from unscrewing during mounting of the work. The screw should protrude about ⅜ in. from the face of the block.

VACUUM CHUCKS

The vacuum chuck is a nifty chuck that is particularly useful for high-production work but is also very good for one-off items, especially bowls. To build a vacuum chuck, you need a vacuum source. There are several ways to create a vacuum. The best way is a vacuum pump, but a good, new pump is expensive—$300 to $500. It is sometimes possible to find used or surplus vacuum pumps designed for the printing and refrigeration industries for less than $100 (see Surplus Center in Resources on p. 185).

If you own an air compressor, you can buy a venturi unit that will make a vacuum from compressed air (see the photo below). The quality

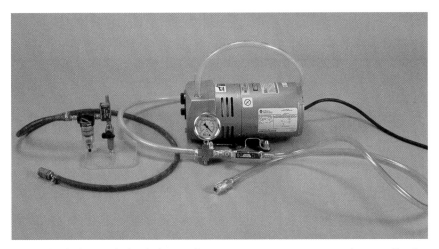

A venturi unit that can be hooked to an air compressor or a vacuum pump is one option for supplying vacuum.

Clead Christiansen's E-Z Vacuum Adapter allows both shop-built and commercial vacuum chucks to be used on any lathe

and price of venturi units vary greatly as does the volume of air required to run them. In general, the higher-priced units require a lower volume of air to maintain a vacuum, with the best units running well from a nail-gun compressor (3 cfm or less).

Another option is to use a shop vacuum, but they don't work very well. First, they are noisy, which disturbs the state of tranquility you are trying to reach by turning. Second, a shop vac does not create sufficient vacuum to have good holding power, and the suction is further diminished by the fact that the vacuum motor will burn up if you completely seal the system. You must leave a small hole for the shop vac to breathe. The result is that you get only 14 in. to 20 in. of mercury from a shop vac (a perfect vacuum is just a tad shy of 30 in. of mercury). With a venturi, you can get 20 in. to 25 in., and a pump will generally give you at least 24 in.

The vacuum chuck is a fairly old idea in turning (shop-built examples date back to the 1950s), but it has really taken off in the last few years. This is mainly due to an inexpensive adapter designed and built by North Ogden, Utah, turner and entrepreneur Clead Christiansen. The problem with vacuum chucks has always been how to get the vacuum through the headstock spindle and into the chuck. A shop-built adapter entailed a lot of work, typically requiring the services of a machine shop. Clead's E-Z Vacuum Adapter solves the problem so elegantly that you can only think, "Gee, I wish I had thought of that!"

The E-Z Vacuum Adapter sells for about $75 and is composed of three pieces. A hub with a standard quick-connect air-compressor fitting set in a router bearing is placed on the outboard end of the headstock spindle. It

A Shop-Built Vacuum Chuck

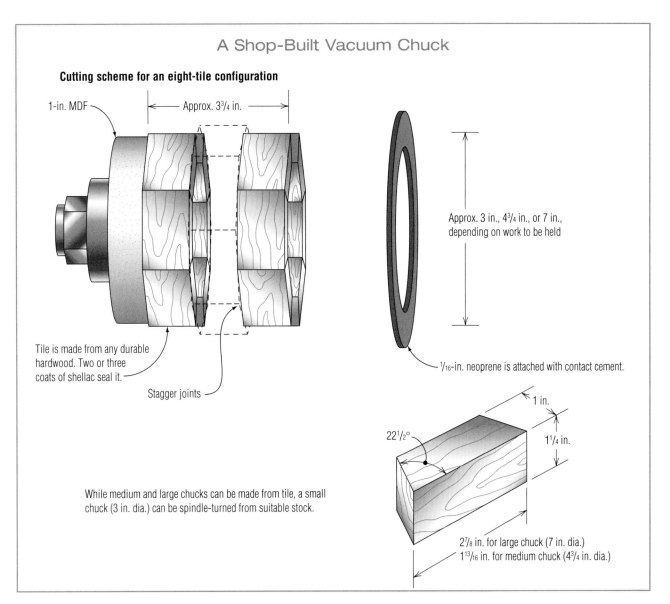

Cutting scheme for an eight-tile configuration

1-in. MDF

Approx. 3³/₄ in.

Tile is made from any durable
hardwood. Two or three
coats of shellac seal it.

Stagger joints

Approx. 3 in., 4³/₄ in., or 7 in.,
depending on work to be held

¹/₁₆-in. neoprene is attached with contact cement.

1 in.

1¹/₄ in.

22¹/₂°

While medium and large chucks can be made from tile, a small
chuck (3 in. dia.) can be spindle-turned from suitable stock.

2⁷/₈ in. for large chuck (7 in. dia.)
1¹³/₁₆ in. for medium chuck (4³/₄ in. dia.)

The beauty of this design is that it will hold
the inside and outside of bowls as well as
flat objects such as platters.

Oneway makes a nice line of vacuum chucks as well as its own rotary vacuum adapter. It also sells vacuum pumps.

has a 60° taper to center it in the spindle. Setting the air-compressor fitting in a router bearing allows the headstock spindle to rotate, while the fitting (and the vacuum hose connected to it) remains stationary. The nose assembly is placed in the spindle nose and has vents to deliver the vacuum to the chuck. It also has a centering point that can be adjusted to any height or removed altogether depending on the needs of the chucking situation.

Connecting the two parts and carrying the vacuum through the spindle is a piece of standard ½-in. lamp rod. The beauty of the lamp rod is that it can be hacksawed to any length so it can accommodate any length spindle. (After sawing, it is best to square the cut and lightly chamfer the thread start on the grinder.) A length of lamp rod comes with the chuck, but you can purchase replacement lengths at any hardware store. The vacuum hose is connected to the adapter with a standard air-line quick connector.

The vacuum chuck itself can take almost any form according to the needs of the chucking situation. It is easy to make a custom vacuum chuck for a production situation and discard it later. Vacuum chucks are most popular with bowl turners, and I have made a shop-built chuck that will handle a wide variety of chucking situations (see the illustration on p. 67). Oneway makes commercial equivalents of this chuck in three sizes, which work very well. It also sells vacuum pumps and its own rotary vacuum spindle adapters. Since you can make essentially the same chuck yourself for the price of a faceplate in less than an hour, it is time well spent.

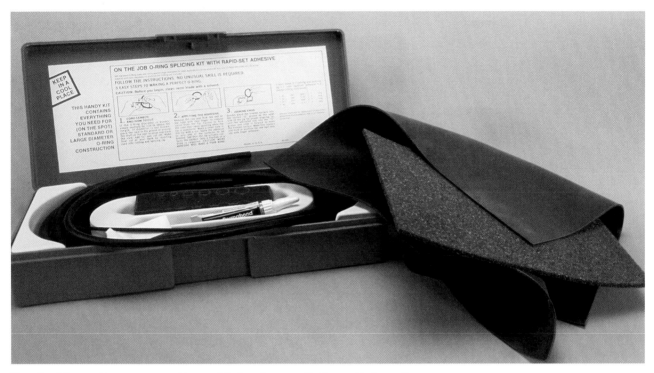

Closed-cell foam rubber, neoprene rubber, and O-rings form an effective seal between the work and a shop-built vacuum chuck. Closed-cell foam needs to be thin (1/16 in. or less) and resilient, while 1/16-in.-thick neoprene works best.

Although turning a suitable wood chuck to hold any item is straight-forward, getting a working seal between the work and the chuck is problematic. Rubber or neoprene gasket material is required. Most turners find that foam (either rubber or neoprene) works, but it must be thin, resilient closed-cell foam to work. Do not use a thick piece of foam because it allows movement of the workpiece, inviting a catch. Self-adhesive weather-stripping (available at any hardware store) also works well for special chucks. I find that 1/16-in.-thick neoprene works best because you can cut it to any size and shape, and it forms to concave and convex chuck surfaces well and is highly resilient. Once cut to shape, the neoprene can be affixed to the chuck with plastic-laminate adhesive or spray adhesive.

Another viable sealing material is a neoprene O-ring. Any bearing supplier and many auto parts stores sell do-it-yourself O-ring kits. Selling for about $25, the kit includes 7 ft. of O-ring material in four sizes (0.103 in., 0.139 in., 0.210 in., and 0.275 in.), a splicing jig, and glue to effect the splice. Using this kit, it is easy to scrape an O-ring groove at the contact point between the chuck and the work and to make an O-ring to fit in it. All wood has some porosity, but a couple of coats of shellac will plug any leakage. Paste wax is good to keep the O-ring in the groove and provide further sealing at this point.

Quick and Easy Centering

Get into the habit of putting a small pencil dot at the center of the work just before transferring it to the vacuum chuck. This practice makes centering child's play because you can touch the dot with the tailstock center before turning on the vacuum.

Once made, the vacuum chuck is fun to use. Simply place the work in the chuck and turn on the vacuum. As with paper joints, you need sufficient vacuum area in relation to the size and weight of the work. A good rule of thumb is a minimum of 10 sq. in. of area, which would give approximately 135 lb. of pressure at 28 in. of mercury but only 100 lb. at 20 in. of mercury. A 10-sq.-in. area works out to a 3⅝-in.-dia. circle inside the gasket. A 3⅝-in. circle may not, however, have sufficient diameter to give a stable hold for work much larger in diameter than the chuck or with a poor vacuum source. Common sense is required here, and keeping the periphery of the chuck to about one-third the diameter of the work is good shop practice. Also keep speeds low to moderate when using these chucks.

JACOBS CHUCKS

Correctly called a "drill chuck," the Jacobs chuck is an old stalwart that is more often named for its original American manufacturer. The head of this chuck has an outer ring and an inner ring that encloses the jaws. Turning the outer ring with a key causes the jaws to open and close. The drill chuck mounts into the lathe on a Morse-taper shaft, which is actually a separate piece that fits into the back of the chuck on a short Jarno taper. Morse-taper "backs" can be purchased in any combination of Morse and Jarno tapers. If you have a drill chuck that does not fit your lathe, you can buy replacement backs from any machine-tool supplier. Also, smaller tapers can be adapted to larger spindle sockets by using taper-sleeve adapters.

The main use for drill chucks is to hold drill bits in either the headstock or the tailstock, but they can also be used to grip small work such as knobs and miniature turnings. Drill chucks are sold according to the largest diameter they can grip. Common sizes are ⅜ in. and ½ in., with the latter being better for woodturning lathes.

FOUR-JAW SCROLL CHUCKS

Scroll chucks are crossovers from metalworking. A steel body encases four jaws that open or close in unison by the action of a circular scroll plate (see the illustration on the facing page). The jaws grip around the end of the workpiece. In metalworking chucks, the scroll plate is typically actuated by means of a key acting through bevel gears. To save expense, woodturning scroll chucks are often made without the bevel gears, instead using steel levers that fit into holes in the two halves of the chuck body to allow turning the scroll plate directly. The Nova and small Oneway chucks operate this way.

How a Scroll Chuck Works

Screw

Top jaw

Most manufacturers make a wide assortment of top jaws for a variety of purposes.

Bottom jaw

The jaw slides in keyway by the action of the scroll plate.

Keyway

Chuck body

Scroll plate

Turning the scroll plate with tommy bars moves the bottom jaws in and out of chuck body.

Snap ring holds scroll in chuck body.

Tommy bars

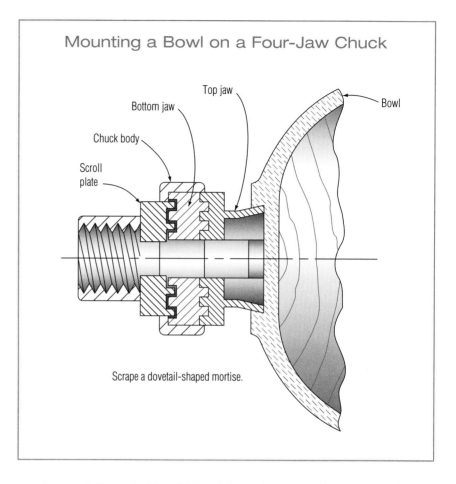

Mounting a Bowl on a Four-Jaw Chuck

Top jaw

Bottom jaw

Bowl

Chuck body

Scroll plate

Scrape a dovetail-shaped mortise.

Oneway's Stronghold and Nova's Super Nova chucks use a novel approach—a key fits in a hole in the chuck body and in effect becomes a bevel gear. This affords much greater leverage in tightening the chuck.

For woodturning, a four-jaw scroll chuck is much more satisfactory than the three-jaw variety because four jaws will grip squares nicely. Although you may be tempted to use a surplus metalturning chuck, it doesn't work as well. Even if the metalworking chuck is of the four-jaw variety, the jaws are not designed for holding wood. They're too small and tend to indent wood without ever centering it. The jaws are real knuckle-busters, too.

Scroll chucks made specifically for woodturning have jaws that hold over a much greater surface area. The top half of the jaws can be unscrewed so that a variety of jaws can be used, each holding a range of sizes (grip range). On some scroll chucks, four plates with numerous tapped holes in their face can be mounted in place of the jaws. By screwing rubber posts to the plates at strategic positions, you can hold odd shapes. For example, you can hold a nearly finished bowl by the rim so that the base can be turned. I call these rubber baby bumper jaws.

Regardless of the maker, rubber baby bumper jaws do not hold well. They cannot be used for primary turning and are only of value for turning away the chucking marks on the bottom of an open-shaped bowl. I can typically mount a disk of plywood on a screw chuck and scrape a groove that is a press fit with the rim much faster than I can change the jaws over and arrange the baby bumpers on the correct circle for the hold. (A vacuum chuck works far better for this purpose.)

Scroll chucks are quick and easy to use and leave no screw holes. If used within the grip range of the jaws, they don't significantly indent the wood. They're ideal for holding small furniture parts such as knobs and finials. A handy way to turn small parts is to feed a standard-sized dowel through the headstock spindle then through the chuck itself. (The advantage of using a dowel for turning is that it doesn't have to be trued round first.) As each small piece is finished and cut off, the dowel can be advanced through the chuck, ready for turning the next piece.

Woodturners tend to think of scroll chucks as gripping by compressing around the outside of the work, but the chucks can also be expanded inside a recess in the work, which could be a pedestal, a bowl, or a small tabletop. Woodturning scroll chucks are angled on the outside faces of the jaws. If a dovetailed (undercut) recess is scraped in the work, the chuck can be expanded to hold securely. This is one of the scroll chuck's most useful features.

All of the chuck makers offer (usually in the standard package) a screw that turns the scroll chuck into a heavy screw chuck. This is one of the handiest accessories for a screw chuck. You can use the screw chuck to grab a bowl blank for the turning of the outside and scraping of a dovetail recess in the foot (base). You can then grab the dovetail recess with a set of jaws of the proper grip range for the turning of the inside of the bowl (see the illustration on the facing page). Now, you can convert back to a screw chuck and grab a disk of plywood to jam-chuck the rim and turn away the dovetail recess. Since you can generally grab the screw without removing the primary jaws, this makes for quick holding.

Safety concerns with scroll chucks are twofold. First, the spinning jaws present an ever-present danger. At best, they're knuckle-busters; at worst, they can maim. Second, inadvertently extending a jaw beyond the grip of the scroll will cause one or more jaws to go ballistic when you start the lathe. Most scroll chucks have a safety feature that prevents this, but it's still a good habit never to extend the jaw more than halfway out of the chuck body. I once overextended the jaws of a scroll chuck when using a metal lathe. A 9-lb. jaw ricocheted off the lathe carriage, went through a Thermopane window, and landed 10 ft. from the building. I've never disobeyed the halfway rule since.

If you are turning with the jaws outside the chuck, it's a good idea to wrap the jaw area with duct tape. The tape softens sharp corners and prevents fingers from getting into the recesses between the jaws.

COMMERCIALLY AVAILABLE SCROLL CHUCKS

Manufacturer	Model	Size	Method of operation
Axminster	Carlton	4 in.	Lever
Axminster	Precision 4-Jaw	4 in.	Key
Latalex Ltd.	Nova (standard)	3½ in.	Lever
Latalex Ltd.	Super Nova	4 in.	Key
Oneway Mfg.	Scroll	4 in.	Lever
Oneway Mfg.	Talon	3½ in.	Key
Oneway Mfg.	Stronghold	4½ in.	Key
Vicmarc	VM 140	6 in.	Lever
Vicmarc	VM 120	5½ in.	Key
Vicmarc	VM 090	3½ in.	Lever
Vicmarc	VM 100	3½ in.	Key

Manufacturers offer a variety of jaws for their chucks. Right now, Nova is the only chuck that allows the jaws to be switched between the lever and key chucks. All of the Nova lever jaws may be used on the Super Nova, however, there is one new set of jaws for the Super Nova that cannot be used on the lever. For those who already own a lever Nova and want to upgrade, the Super Nova is sold sans jaws at a cheaper price.

You need to look at more than just the price of a chuck. Cost out the basic chuck and all of the jaws you think you will need to get a fair comparison. The jaws run up the price of a chuck rapidly. Finally, don't think a scroll chuck will be a panacea to your holding problems. I use scroll chucks but not all that much. Learn to use centers, faceplates, and jam chucks *before* rushing out to buy a scroll chuck.

Accessories

I suppose you could live without accessories, but at least for me they are part of the fun of turning. Since you can build many accessories in the shop, you don't necessarily have to part with a lot of cash either. If your pockets are deep, the accessories can be as much fun as the turning. In short, I have never met an accessory that I didn't enjoy trying, and there are many that I wouldn't be without.

Steady Rests

There comes a point where a spindle is so long and thin that the only way to prevent chatter is to use a steady rest to support the work. Many modern turners have great misconceptions about steady rests because they associate them with rests used in metalturning. In metalturning, the tool is mounted on a carriage that rides along the bed ways of the machine, so the rest must support the work on exact center to avoid turning a taper. This requires surrounding the work with plane bearings or ball bearings for support.

In woodturning, the tool is guided by the turner, and exact centering by the steady rest is unimportant. A woodturning steady rest must be able to dampen vibration, support the work to prevent it from bending away from the tool, and be quick to adjust.

As with chucks, I feel that the best steady rest is one that you make yourself. My plan for a steady rest, shown in the illustration on p. 76, closely follows one outlined by Frank Pain in his book *Practical*

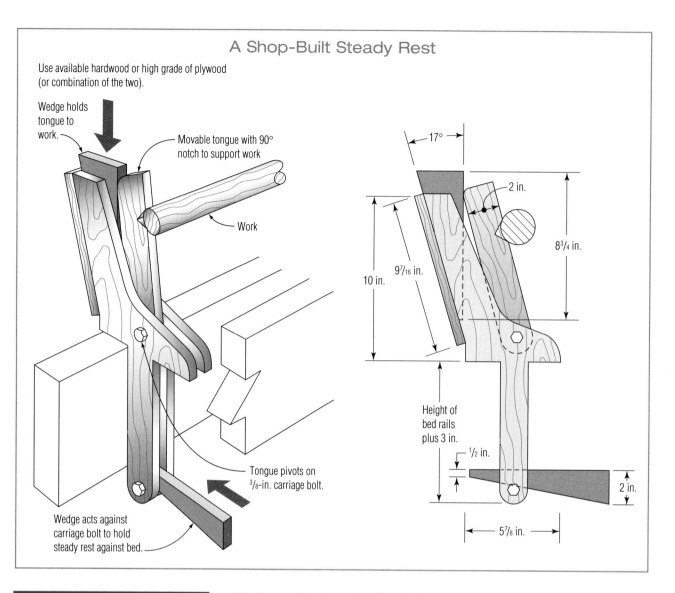

A Shop-Built Steady Rest

Use available hardwood or high grade of plywood
(or combination of the two).

Wedge holds
tongue to
work.

Movable tongue with 90°
notch to support work

Work

Tongue pivots on
3/8-in. carriage bolt.

Wedge acts against
carriage bolt to hold
steady rest against bed.

17°

2 in.

8 3/4 in.

9 7/16 in.

10 in.

Height of
bed rails
plus 3 in.

1/2 in.

2 in.

5 7/8 in.

Avoiding a Bow

One problem with long turnings is that no matter how carefully the stock was jointed and planed, a bit of bow sets in with any change in humidity. The solution is simple. All turnings tend to taper to one end or the other. Merely offset the small end from center to get the turning centered between the big end and the steady.

Woodturner (Sterling, 1990), which in turn is based on an early steady rest in the High Wycombe Museum in England. Except for the mention in Pain's book, the design has been largely forgotten, and today's commercial steady rests trace their roots to metalturning.

The shop-built steady can be positioned at any point along the bed of the lathe and be secured by a wood wedge. The metal beds on some lathes may make this mounting system impractical. In such instances, a block under the bed ways with a carriage bolt and a nut to secure the steady is a good substitute. The movable tongue can be adjusted quickly to any size workpiece by raising and lowering the top wedge.

If the wedge has a tendency to work loose, Pain suggests adding lead weight to the top of it. I have found that a second slender wedge driven beside the first locks the wedge at the desired height. To cut the 90° notch in the top wedge, simply mount a $\frac{1}{16}$-in. drill bit in the headstock, set the steady on the bed, and touch the movable tongue to the drill. Bandsaw a 90° corner at the drill mark, and the notch is at perfect center height for your lathe. Once in place, the steady may still have to be fine-tuned by chiseling one side of the notch a bit to get both sides to give equal pressure to the spindle.

The advantage of this steady is that you can turn right through it, and it quickly readjusts to support the work at the new diameter. If you find that the workpiece becomes hot and starts to burn as it rubs against the sides of the notch, slow down the lathe and add a little candle wax to provide lubrication. Mechanically fastening (I use carpet tacks) a patch of nylon or Teflon to the notch area will also work. This steady works best at rather slow speed (around 1,100 rpm for most spindle work), but this lower speed deals better with harmonic chatter and is far superior for skew work.

In my experience, although all turners know that a steady rest is needed at times to overcome harmonic chatter, very few of them use one. Most turners just live with the chatter and sand it out at the end. I believe that a steady rest is indispensable in spindle turning, whether you're making one part or many. The couple of hours spent making a steady will be repaid many times by better work, less sanding, and less frustration.

Arm Rests

The arm rest is an auxiliary tool rest that saves you from having to move your main tool rest when you're working on the face of the work. An added advantage of the arm rest is that it allows you to quickly obtain center height for the tool. At the very center of the work, the tool must

An arm rest saves fiddling with the tool rest. It can quickly be brought into play to support a tool, typically a scraper. Raising or lowering your shoulder adjusts the rest height, so a tool can be brought to the center of the work almost instantly.

Turning Long, Thin Spindles

To start, find a point near the middle of the turning that is either straight or slightly tapered. Set up the steady rest at this position, making sure it is firmly attached to the bed. Now establish a diameter about ¹/₁₆ in. larger in diameter than the actual turning at this point. This essentially forms a plane bearing around the work for the steady to ride on. Throughout this sequence, my lathe was running at about 1,000 rpm.

1 Place the billet in the lathe between exact centers, and take a light cut in the middle with a roughing-out gouge. If you only cut on one or two corners, you need to offset a bit. Once you've offset the billet, do another trial cut to ensure that the stock is being removed equally from all four corners.

2 Turn the spindle round in the area of the steady rest. Don't rough more than just this area because you need the extra strength provided by the square section to keep harmonic chatter to a minimum while you turn a bearing surface.

3 Using calipers and a cutoff tool, size to the final diameter of the spindle to each side of the steady rest.

4 With a light touch, use the roughing-out gouge to true up the area between the two parting-tool cuts. I hold the work in my left hand while holding the tool down on the rest with my left thumb to dampen vibration during this critical cut.

5 Start up the lathe, then apply some paraffin.

6 Push down the wedge until the spindle is deflected just a bit, and lock the main wedge in place with the secondary locking wedge.

7 Work from the largest diameters to the smallest. Because of the steady, my skew cuts beautifully without harmonic chatter. To size the end of my baluster to ½ in., I use a ½-in. open-end wrench as a ready-set caliper. Finally, trim away the bearing surface under the steady with a skew.

8 Remove the wedge from the steady and sand.

9 The finished spindle "right off the tools."

be exactly on-center, and any inaccuracies can be corrected instantly by raising or lowering your shoulder.

The first time I saw an arm rest was in the hands of fourth-generation master turner Dick Bailey. It struck me as such a good idea that I went home and made one myself. Fortunately, they are now available commercially. Still, it is an easy tool to make yourself, since it's essentially a bent piece of structural steel.

To use an arm rest, place its handle under your left arm and the shank on the tool rest, then set your turning tool in the hook of the arm rest. Most of the controlling of the tool is done using the right hand, but the left hand can move the tool in and out by sliding the arm rest in the same directions on the rest. The arm rest is most often used with scrapers for making chucks and is essential for chasing inside threads (see pp. 145–146). It should not be used with roughing gouges or skew chisels.

Sharpening Equipment

Sharpening is the most difficult part of learning to turn. It is especially hard to sort out on your own because you just don't know where to start and you do not have a properly sharpened tool with which to compare your efforts. The same skills and motions required to actually turn are necessary to sharpen (albeit in reverse or mirror image). But wait a minute, you may not have learned to turn yet. Adding insult to injury, you can't learn to turn unless a sharp tool is placed in your hands. Which came first: the chicken or the egg, turning or sharpening?

I have come to the conclusion that it is not difficult for anyone to become proficient at woodturning if a sharp tool is placed in his or her hands. The concept of how a turning tool cuts is easy to grasp, and the execution only takes a bit of practice. The reason more people are not proficient turners is that they don't start out with a sharp tool.

By sharp, I mean really sharp, sharp enough to shave hair off your arm. But a sharp turning tool entails much more than this because I have had numerous students bring tools that shaved hair but did not turn wood. In addition to being sharp, the tool must also be of the correct shape and have the correct grind angles on the bevels (see the illustration on p. 115). This is a tall order, since most turning tools are not delivered sharp or with the correct grind angles. Most are not even the right shape. This is why I have included illustrations of each turning tool in chapter 6. You can compare your tool with the appropriate illustration to better see whether you have the correct grind angles.

When I first discovered woodturning, I had to learn to sharpen freehand, which added time and difficulty to the learning curve. Today there are a number of good, reasonably priced jigs that take 80 percent of the freehand skill out of the sharpening equation. I teach jigs in all of my turn-

---

Keeping an Arm Rest Handy

Drill a hole in the end of the handle of your arm rest. You can loop a cord through the hole and hang the rest under your left shoulder where it will always be ready for instant use.

ing classes, and every student can sharpen his or her own tools within half a day. When I had to teach freehand, I was lucky if two out of eight students got the hang of sharpening in five days. While I can still sharpen freehand, I now elect to use the jig because I get perfect symmetrical grinds (the same angles on both sides of a tool). I recommend that you start with a jig as well.

Sharpening can be divided into three distinct operations: establishing the correct shape and bevel angles, grinding when the tools become dull, and honing. The establishment of the correct shape and bevel angles is really a heavy grinding operation; after the correct shape is obtained, only light grinding is necessary to maintain the tool. Honing makes the ground edge really sharp. I'll look at the equipment needed for each of these operations in detail.

GRINDERS

Bench grinders for home and light-industrial use come in 6-in., 7-in., 8-in., and 10-in. sizes. The smaller three sizes are generally built on a 3,450-rpm motor frame, while the 10-in. one is constructed on a 1,725-rpm frame. Many think the larger machine emits less heat because of the slower speed, but there is really not much difference. A 6-in. grinding wheel at 3,450 rpm has a surface speed of 5,416 ft. per minute, while a 10-in. wheel running at 1,725 rpm goes 4,516 ft. per minute. Several companies offer 6-in. grinders built on a 1,725-rpm motor, which gives a surface speed of 2,710 ft. per minute.

Economy bench grinders typically come with fixed, one-piece cast rests, which allow grinding only at 90°. That means aftermarket or shop-built rests and jig systems are necessary to grind turning tools effectively.

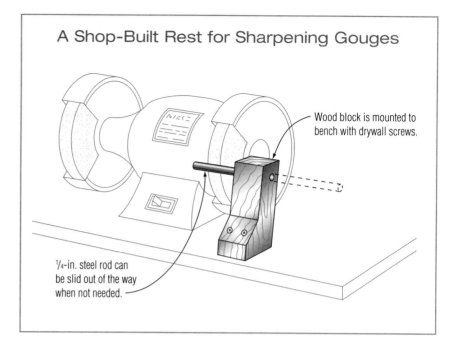

A Shop-Built Rest for Sharpening Gouges

Wood block is mounted to bench with drywall screws.

¼-in. steel rod can be slid out of the way when not needed.

Although many tout the virtues of low-speed grinding, there is actually a loss of efficiency at surface speeds much below 4,000 ft. per minute. Because things happen more slowly, though, you'll have more control, which is why beginners are more comfortable with these machines. If you are going to use a jig to sharpen your tools, a normal speed, 8-in. grinder works best. A low-speed grinder would only waste time because sharpening takes longer.

Because it is difficult to rock a tool up off of a flat table when freehand grinding, many turners like to fabricate a rest for grinding gouges that emulates the tool rest on their lathes (see the illustration above). This idea makes sense because the movements of freehand sharpening are somewhat similar to those of actual turning. For an experienced grinder, this is the best rest for sharpening gouges freehand, but with it you have no way to judge that the bevel angle is correct. Fortunately, the process is actually self-regulating. When the angle becomes too acute, the tool gets catchy and the edge wears too quickly. When the angle becomes too obtuse, the tool does not cut cleanly and beads become more difficult to roll.

For gouges, a rest that emulates the tool rest on your lathe works best because it allows you to roll the tool easily to create the complex shape required of a bowl or combination gouge. You must learn to turn on the grinder, set the tool on the rest, slide it forward into the wheel, and immediately start moving it laterally. This is easy to do with roughing gouges, parting tools, and scrapers but difficult with spindle, combination, and bowl gouges.

Grinder Safety

GRINDERS ARE AN OLD SHOP workhorse, but there are a number of safety concerns connected with them. Let's take a look at how to grind safely.

Safety Shields

Make it a habit to view grinding activity through the glass or plastic viewing shield because it provides a second barrier of protection (in addition to your eyewear) should the wheel disintegrate. Traditionally, the safety shields on any grinder were metal frames with tempered safety glass in them—two layers of tempered safety glass with a sheet of plastic in between. This "sandwich" creates a nearly shatterproof, scratch-resistant surface.

Most grinders today are supplied with plastic viewing shields, which reduces manufacturing costs. If your grinder has plastic shields in a frame, consider replacing it with a glass/plastic sandwich. If you must make do with plastic, some antistatic spray from a computer shop helps to repel dust.

Lighting

Good lighting at a grinder is a must! Although industrial grinders often have lighting built into the safety-shield frames, economy grinders leave lighting to the end user. You'll need a simple gooseneck lamp for direct local lighting.

Guards

Any grinder should provide guarding that encloses the wheel except at the area just above the rest. An open, unguarded wheel should be avoided under all circumstances. Most grinders have a sliding shield called a spark arrestor at the top edge of the guard. In addition to reducing the number of sparks that land on your hands during grinding, the spark arrestor helps to contain shrapnel inside the guards should the wheel explode. You should slide the spark arrestors to within $\frac{1}{16}$ in. of the wheel, and as the wheel is dressed, you should readjust them.

Eyewear

Safety glasses are obviously a must around any grinding equipment. If your glasses are not true safety glasses with side shields, then you'll need goggles or a face shield.

New wheels

A good practice with a new wheel, whether it is a replacement or one on a new grinder, is to tap it to see how it rings. Like a baseball bat, it will not ring true if it is cracked. When you mount a new wheel in the grinder, it is best to stand to one side, start the machine, and leave the room for a few minutes. If there is a defect in the wheel, it will typically disintegrate at or shortly after startup. Never start the grinder without all guards securely in place.

Grinding wheels Most grinders are delivered with silicon-carbide wheels (available in most hardware stores). Such wheels are good for grinding almost anything from steel to glass or even bathroom tiles, but they grind too hot for tool steel. A better choice for tool grinding is an aluminum-oxide wheel. Often called pink wheels, they are just as often blue or white. An aluminum-oxide wheel has a bonding medium that is softer than that of the silicon-carbide wheel, which helps create the right amount of friability. Friability means to crumble. "Why would anyone pay extra for grinding wheels that crumble?" you ask. Because it makes the wheel self-sharpening and self-cleaning. Old, worn particles break off, which in turn brings up fresh sharp ones.

The trick is to find the correct amount of friability so that the wheel is not excessively soft and will only shed particles as they become dull. An aluminum-oxide wheel's code number will start with A (for aluminum oxide) followed by the grit (36, 80, 100, and so on), then a letter indicating the friability. The letters A through G indicate very soft wheels that crumble easily, while the letters H through K represent soft wheels in the range that is useful for sharpening woodworking tools. The letters P through S appear on hard wheels, and letters beyond that are very hard wheels.

In general, an H or I wheel has about the right friability for general woodturning-tool grinding, as well as for carbon-steel tools such as plane irons and bench chisels. For exclusive use on high-speed steel (HSS), many turners prefer a harder wheel in the J or even K range. These harder wheels are more aggressive and work well for initial shaping of HSS (I use an A46K wheel for initial shaping of new tools). Without great care, however, harder wheels will burn carbon steel.

Aluminum-oxide wheels can be found at industrial-tool suppliers. Friability standards are a voluntary trade standard and can vary from manufacturer to manufacturer. Once you find a brand you like, stick with it.

The vibration levels of many bench grinders may make them difficult to use—especially if the grinder is lightweight. Dressing with a diamond dresser usually improves this situation, but it seldom eliminates vibration altogether. If the grinder is not clamped to a bench, it will walk away. The principal culprit here is the average grinding wheel, which is often out of balance. How out of balance it is depends on the wheel. Norton wheels, for instance, tend to be very good, while the Chinese wheels that came on my imported grinder are horrible. It pays to buy a good wheel.

You can improve your grinder's performance by installing Oneway hubs, but you will have to buy new wheels with larger arbor holes to accept the hubs. The hubs have a series of threaded holes that accept set screws as counterweights. The manufacturer's directions suggest balancing the wheel, then dressing it (with its fixture), then balancing it again. The result is that a Canadian faceted penny, which is supplied with the balancing weights, will stand on edge on top of the grinder. Grinding is a joy: The grinder just sits on the bench and purrs. With these advantages, a Oneway balancing system is worth consideration.

Quenching Carbon Steel

When you grind carbon-steel tools, keep a good-sized quenching tub next to the grinder. A metal tub is best because a hot tool can burn through the bottom of a plastic tub.

By installing new wheels with Oneway's hubs on your grinder, it is possible to balance the wheels, which will remove all vibration and make grinding easier.

Most people make the mistake of grinding with too fine a wheel. A good roughing wheel is 46 to 60 grit, while the finishing wheel should be 80 to 120 grit. For dry grinding, you should never use finer than 150 grit. Remember that the grit you select for grinding wheels should never be as coarse as what you would typically select for hand-sanding, which is how most woodworkers typically judge grit. This is because each particle of abrasive has less penetration when moving at speed.

Dressing wheels A new grinding wheel, whether it comes with the grinder or is a replacement, is about as round as a freshly mounted turning billet. It is impossible to grind well on such a wheel because the work will just hop up and down. Therefore, some means of truing your grinding wheel is as important as the grinder itself. Truing can be broken down into two operations. The first is the actual truing, that is, making the wheel concentric with the grinding machine's arbor and making the face of the wheel square (90° to the sides of the wheel). The second operation is dressing.

Dressing is done to give the wheel the desired texture and to bring up sharp new particles when necessary. Only about 10 percent of the particles in a given wheel actually cut—the rest just rub. As you grind, the 10 percent of the particles that are doing the work dull. The area between them fills up with metal, causing the particles effectively to lose their clearance. The wheel needs to be dressed to sharpen and clean it. Dressing must be done any time you can see steel in the surface of the wheel, when the surface looks glazed, or when the wheel has grooves worn in it. It has to be done more frequently with a hard wheel than with a soft one.

Several accessories to true and dress are available. The best method to true the wheel is by using a diamond dresser, preferably in combination with some sort of jig to ensure that the wheel is dressed square as well as round. A diamond dresser is no more than an industrial diamond brazed into the end of a piece of cold-rolled steel. By setting the shank on the grinding rest and sliding the diamond tip laterally across the grinding wheel, the wheel will become round. The diamond dresser should be presented with a fairly light touch at a 5° negative (downhill) angle to the face of the wheel in a scrape cut. The Oneway dressing attachment does this automatically and dresses the wheel round and square to boot (see the photo below). If you don't have a jig, it is easy to tilt the table a bit downhill and use it to support a standard dresser.

Buying a diamond dresser is like buying a diamond ring—the size dictates the price. Fortunately, industrial diamonds are cheap compared with their aristocratic gem-quality cousins. A good diamond dresser will cost you between $15 and $60. Bigger dressers, called clusters, contain more

The Oneway dressing attachment presents the diamond dresser to the wheel at the correct 5° negative (downhill) angle and ensures that the wheel is dressed true to its axis.

than one diamond and are typically in the $60 price range. Clusters, however, are not good for truing a wheel with a jig because they leave a finish similar to that left by a star-wheel dresser. Diamond dressers are available from industrial-supply houses, so pick one up when you are buying your aluminum-oxide wheels.

A star-wheel dresser, which is available at any hardware store, is good to use in combination with a diamond dresser. Since a star-wheel dresser follows the contour of a wheel, it does not really make it round—only a diamond can do that. But a star-wheel dresser does give the wheel a much rougher texture than a diamond, so it is great for dressing your coarse wheel (after it is made round with a diamond) in preparation for the initial shaping of new tools. A star-dressed wheel is much more aggressive than a diamond-dressed wheel, removing metal fast with a minimum of heat. After about two dressings with a star wheel, the wheel will be out of round and you'll need to use the diamond dresser again.

The worst type of dresser is a silicon-carbide stick. These sticks are only marginally harder than the wheel, so they leave a glazed surface that tends to grind hot.

HONING EQUIPMENT

A truly sharp edge is formed when two flat planes (or an arc and a flat plane) meet perfectly with a good surface finish at the cutting edge. A good surface finish may be defined as a polish or near polish. Honing leaves a polished or near polished edge free of feather (or burr). In short, your spindle-turning tool should be razor sharp after honing.

There are two methods by which I hone lathe tools—whetstones and buffing. If at all possible, I buff because it's the fastest, most effective method. I only resort to whetstones when absolutely necessary, such as when working in someone else's shop. The one tool that is an exception is the skew chisel, which I always hone on whetstones. In fact, barring nicking the edge on a chuck or dropping it on a concrete floor, stones are the only way I sharpen a skew. This is because the skew works best with an absolutely flat bevel and must have a keen edge.

Whetstones As the name implies, whetstones are used with oil or water, which acts as a lubricant to prevent metal particles from bonding into the pores of the stone. Honing lathe tools requires polishing stones with very fine grit. Although I sharpen my skew chisels on the same stones that I use for plane irons and bench chisels, I have a collection of odd-shaped stones for the rest of my turning tools. These include small, tapered stones called slips and a variety of stones in triangular, round, and knife-edge designs. The latter are often sold in catalogs as files, but they are actually stones.

The trick to using flat stones to sharpen skew chisels is to keep the bevel absolutely flat on the stone. A honing jig can be of great help here. Most of the jigs that are used for honing plane blades and bench chisels can be adapted for honing a skew (see the illustration on p. 129). The advantage to a jig is that you will obtain a flat bevel and a perfect edge.

Over the years, I have collected a wide variety of specialized stones for sharpening turning tools.

For most tools, it is typically easiest to hold the tool in one hand and the stone in the other. View the operation from the side so that you can be sure that the stone is contacting at the edge and at the heel.

If you do not have a jig, you will have to do it by feel. I have observed that most beginners place their hands far back on the tool, often holding chisels by the handle. Instead, you should place the tool down on the heel of the bevel and rock it forward until you feel the bevel go flat on the stone. In this position, you can lock your wrists and stroke in either a circular or a back-and-forth motion to maintain a flat bevel. Since the heel of the bevel is a fulcrum point, the shank of the tool is a lever arm. The farther back you grip, the longer the lever arm and the less you can feel the bevel. If possible, remove the tool handle because its weight throws off your sense of feel.

Whether you use circular motions or linear motions for the actual honing does not make much difference. The important thing is to maintain the bevel flat on the stone by locking your wrists and using your arms and upper body. Start with a sufficiently coarse stone that will remove enough metal to establish a new bevel along the entire cutting edge. Stop every so often and feel if you have rolled a burr along the back of the edge. This will be less or more pronounced depending on the grit of the stone. Work up to the next grade of stone, and keep progressing until you obtain a polish.

For the rest of the tools, it is typically easiest to hold the tool in one hand and the stone in the other. By looking sideways at the process, you can tell if you have placed the stone flat on the bevel (contacting at the edge and heel). I often find it easier to brace the shank of the tool against the headstock or tailstock. This gives me both leverage and steadiness.

For the flute side of gouges, it is just a matter of finding a stone with a radius as close to the flute radius as possible and placing it flat down in the flute (see the illustration at right). Next, remove the burr and polish the edge with a rapid back-and-forth motion. I use plenty of water or oil, as required, during the entire process.

Honing is much easier with hollow-ground edges because the stone will touch at the very edge and the heel of the bevel. It takes a short time to bring up a polished edge. You can normally hone several times before having to go back to the grinder.

Buffers Buffing is the technique of using cloth or felt wheels, which revolve at high speed and are charged with abrasive compound, to improve the surface finish of metal. The abrasive compound is typically a wax/grease and abrasive mixture. Sold in stick form, it is crayoned on the revolving wheel. Many people make a buffer by simply mounting a cloth wheel in a bench grinder. I do not think a bench grinder makes a good buffer because the rest and guards get in the way.

One way to make a small buffer is to mount a buffing wheel in the lathe itself. Small arbors with a ¼-in. or ⅜-in. shank are sold for mounting a 4-in.-dia. buffing wheel in an electric drill. By mounting the arbor in a drill chuck in the headstock spindle of your lathe, you have an inexpensive (less than $20 including the compound) and effective buffer. I first latched onto this idea because I needed a buffer on the road when I do seminars and demonstrations.

In the long run, you will want to build another kind of buffer. Using a buffing wheel mounted in the lathe is inconvenient for tool sharpening because the work must be removed from the lathe every time you want to buff. Several companies manufacture inexpensive arbor heads for the pur-

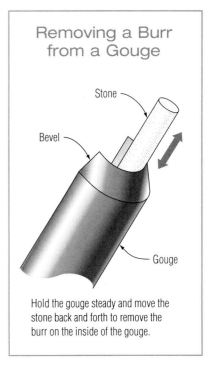

Removing a Burr from a Gouge

Stone

Bevel

Gouge

Hold the gouge steady and move the stone back and forth to remove the burr on the inside of the gouge.

Mount the wheel and arbor in a drill chuck in the lathe.

pose of building a buffer. These arbor heads have a ½-in. arbor, which fits readily available 6-in.-, 8-in.-, and 10-in.-dia. cloth wheels, and are best powered by a ¼-hp or ⅓-hp 1,725-rpm motor. Often a used motor can be found at a motor rewinder for a nominal price. To calculate the correct motor pulley diameter for 6-in. wheels and a 1,725-rpm motor, use the following formula:

$$\text{Motor pulley diameter} = \frac{2,000 \times \text{Arbor head pulley diameter}}{1,725}$$

An rpm of 2,000 is needed to achieve 3,150 surface ft. per minute. For an 8-in.-dia. wheel, use 1,500 rpm instead of 2,000 rpm, and for a 10-in.-dia. wheel, use 1,200 rpm to achieve 3,150 surface ft. per minute. However, these bigger wheels can run even slower if pulley matching is a problem.

Wheels are available in two types: spiral sewn and cushion sewn. The descriptions denote how the layers of cloth that form the wheel are sewn together. As the name implies, the first type is stitched in a spiral starting at the center. The cushion-sewn wheel is stitched in concentric rings, making this type of wheel softer and fluffier. The spiral-sewn wheel is better for coarser compounds where aggressive cutting action is desired, while the cushion-sewn wheel is better for final polishing when gentle cutting action and a mirror finish is the goal.

Buffing compounds tend to be sold according to their final purpose—buffing brass, steel, stainless steel, and so on. Sometimes a compound will do several jobs. For instance, stainless-steel compound is good for final buffing of steel or stainless steel and works well on brass.

For buffing lathe tools, I have found that a combination of two Dico compounds—E5 Emery and SCR Stainless—works well. Dico compounds and buffing wheels are made by Divine Brothers in Utica, N.Y., and are available in most good hardware stores. Equivalent compounds are made

Buffer Motors

An old furnace blower motor is great for powering a shop-built buffer.

by Formax Company in Detroit, Mich., and are sold at all Sears stores. E5 Emery is a fairly aggressive compound that will even remove rust from tools. It is great for initial buffing to remove grind marks and feather.

SCR Stainless is a great final compound to remove all traces of feather and bring the surface to a high polish. It is also good for touching up a slightly dull tool between grindings. I keep a spiral-sewn wheel charged with E5 Emery on the left side of my buffing arbor and a cushion-sewn wheel charged with SCR Stainless on the right. After grinding, I lightly buff on the left wheel, then move to the right wheel for final finishing.

In grinding you always grind into the edge, but when buffing you must *always* buff off of the edge. Buffing into the edge could send you to the emergency room to have a tool removed from your leg. You must also touch the surface you wish to buff tangentially to the wheel (alternately the bevel and the back, or flute) until all feather is removed and a polish is created at the cutting edge. Most people make the mistake of sticking the tool straight into the wheel, which is counterproductive. The goal is to end up with a flat or slightly concave bevel leading to an edge that is free of feather. The key is to keep it light. Heavy buffing with any degree of pressure will round over the edge, requiring a return to the grinder.

For those using a Tormek grinder, honing is done by stropping. The machine comes with a flat strop much the size and shape of a buffing wheel. It is great for the outside of gouges, skew chisels, bedans, beading, and parting tools. For the inside of gouges, the optional profile leather honing wheel is necessary. The leather strops must be charged periodically with a chromium-oxide paste (a tube is supplied with the basic machine). A new strop will eat paste, but you can reduce this tendency by first covering the strops with a liberal amount of mineral oil, then applying the stropping paste.

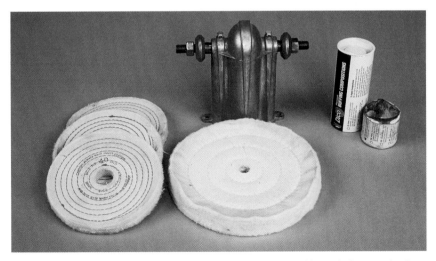

Shown here are arbor heads suitable for making a buffer along with a spiral-sewn wheel (left) and a cushion-sewn wheel (right). Divine Brothers' compounds are shown at the upper right.

Proper buffing technique when honing a spindle gouge requires you to buff off the edge and to hold the tool tangentially to the wheel.

For the inside of gouges, the optional profile honing strop on a Tormek machine mounts outboard on the normal strop supplied with the machine.

SHARPENING JIGS

Grinding is more a matter of practice than anything else, but as I mentioned earlier, a jig greatly simplifies the learning curve. For most people, especially those who may have long hiatuses between turning sessions, a jig is the way to go. I think spindle gouges and bowl gouges come out better shaped and sharper from a jig. I would call myself an accomplished tool grinder, and I cannot grind a spindle or bowl gouge as well as a jig does. An added bonus is that much less steel is removed in the grinding process so the tool lasts longer. With all these overwhelming advantages, jigs are the way I now sharpen my tools.

The Oneway Wolverine grinding jig is the most comprehensive jig for sharpening turning tools. It is the brainchild of Oneway's driving force, Canadian Tim Clay, an avid amateur turner. Tim looked at the entire grinding process and came up with some innovative solutions to old sharpening problems. His approach starts with balancing the wheels, dressing them properly, and using jigs to create perfect geometry.

The basic Wolverine grinding jig comes with two base units that mount under each grinding wheel and an arm that will fit into either base unit (see the photo below). The unit is designed for and works best with an 8-in. grinder. Smaller 6-in. or 7-in. grinders can be blocked up, and a system for 10-in. grinders is available on special request directly from Oneway. There is also a generously sized (3-in. by 5-in.) articulating table that fits into either base unit. This table is great for plane irons and bench chisels as well as turning scrapers.

Also available is the Vari-Grind jig, which does a splendid job of grinding spindle, combination, and bowl gouges to any desired combination of nose and flank angle. Begin by clamping a gouge in the side-grinding jig. In order to repeat a grind perfectly, the gouge must protrude out of the jig the same amount each time. To ensure the right placement, draw a line beside the grinder as a reference point for setting the tool extension. With the grinder stopped, place the tang of the jig in the pocket at the end of the arm, and adjust the arm in or out until the desired nose

Joining Grinder and Jig

Mounting your grinder and sharpening jig on a suitable board makes them portable but maintains the sharpening jig's relationship to the grinder. Put rubber feet (available at most hardware stores) under the board to make the grinder more stable.

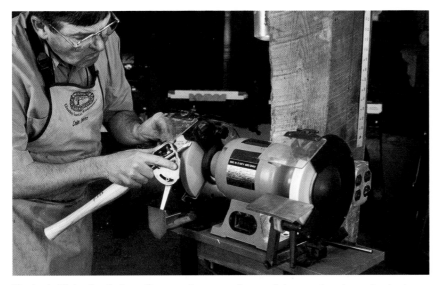

The basic Wolverine jig from Oneway gives you a base unit to mount under each wheel, a tilting table that is good for scrapers, plane irons, and standard woodworking chisels, and an arm (pocket jig) for sharpening roughing gouges and for use with the Vari-Grind jig.

Jig Settings

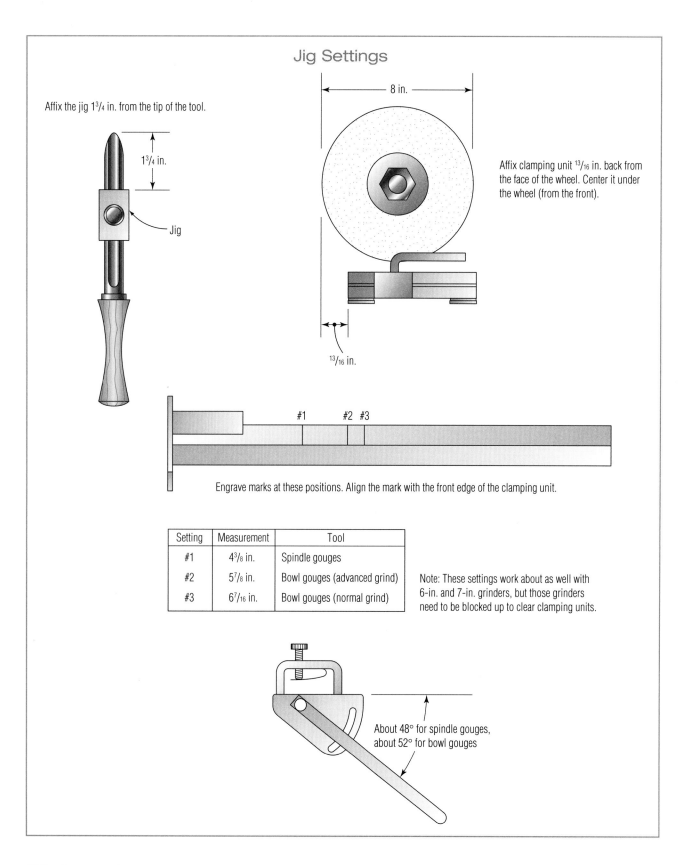

Affix the jig 1³/₄ in. from the tip of the tool.

1³/₄ in.

Jig

8 in.

Affix clamping unit ¹³/₁₆ in. back from the face of the wheel. Center it under the wheel (from the front).

¹³/₁₆ in.

#1   #2 #3

Engrave marks at these positions. Align the mark with the front edge of the clamping unit.

Setting	Measurement	Tool
#1	4³/₈ in.	Spindle gouges
#2	5⁷/₈ in.	Bowl gouges (advanced grind)
#3	6⁷/₁₆ in.	Bowl gouges (normal grind)

Note: These settings work about as well with 6-in. and 7-in. grinders, but those grinders need to be blocked up to clear clamping units.

About 48° for spindle gouges, about 52° for bowl gouges

angle of grind is achieved. The amount of articulation of the jig itself controls the angle of the flanks adjacent to the nose.

Start the grinder, and slowly rotate the tool to achieve the desired shape. While some skill is necessary to achieve the correct shape, the process is so easy that it comes quite naturally. Also a perfect shape is achieved because the tool contacts the wheel in the right place all the time. If you wish to duplicate this grind easily in the future, it is best to engrave marks on the arm with a vibrating engraving tool. I have included my recommended settings for the jigs reviewed here in the illustration on the facing page.

Oneway also makes a jig for grinding skew chisels. Unfortunately, this jig doesn't work well for skew chisels. Following Oneway's directions, you achieve a curved hollow grind, which is wretched for architectural turners. The only way I know to achieve the flat grind is as outlined on p. 126.

The Sorby fingernail profiling jig is the most economical of the jigs. It exhibits beautiful workmanship and finish but comes with rather poor directions. It works with any size grinder and is simple to operate. The disadvantage is that it only works with the wheel you attach in front of it. Any woodworker worth his salt, however, could work out some sort of rapid clamping fixture to locate the jig at either wheel or get it out of the way when not grinding gouges.

For both the Sorby and Oneway jigs, I recommend mounting your grinder on a suitable piece of wood, then attaching the jig to this subbase. This keeps the relationship between the jig and the grinder constant but allows the grinder to be portable. I like to attach four rubber feet to the bottom of this subbase because they absorb vibration and help the grinder to stay put.

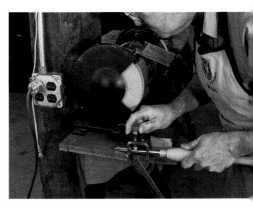

Since the Vari-Grind jig depends on clamping on the top edges of the flute to hold the tool square in the jig, older tools whose flutes are short present a problem. The solution is to grind a flat spot (which is square with the flute) on the tool shank with a right-angle weld grinder.

The Sorby fingernail profiling jig is the most economical fingernail grinding jig. The articulated gooseneck part of this jig is actually built by Tormek for Sorby.

The Tormek SuperGrind sharpening system has a fingernail jig similar to Oneway's. It allows you to grind a wide variety of fingernails on both spindle and bowl gouges. It is a logical choice for those who already own a Tormek.

There is also a fingernail jig for the Tormek SuperGrind sharpening system. The Tormek is a superb low-speed wet grinder for general wood-working tools such as plane irons and bench chisels. With the fingernail jig, the Tormek works for spindle, bowl, and combination gouges. It cannot, however, grind a bowl gouge to a relatively short nose bevel with medium bevels at the flanks—the asymmetrical grind necessary for deep hollow-vessel work. This is a drawback for serious bowl turners, so if you make a lot of bowls consider the Oneway system. If you are a general woodworker who wants to do spindle work and casual faceplate turning, the SuperGrind system is well worth a look, especially if you already own a Tormek.

Another drawback to the Tormek for lathe tools is that it takes a while to initially establish a bevel angle—I find it to be absolutely pokey. Once the geometry is established, however, the time to resharpen the tool is about the same as with a grinder and jig. The Tormek comes with a leather strop as the left wheel, which nicely replaces a buffer for honing. For gouges, you will have to buy the profile leather honing wheel, which mounts outboard of the main strop wheel, to do the flutes.

The Tormek is expensive, but if you do not own any sharpening equipment, it represents a good value because you would spend about the same in the long run for a grinder, jig, buffer, and some sharpening stones. It is an especially good value if you also want to sharpen general woodworking tools.

More than one turner has looked at sharpening jigs and thought, "I could build that myself." That is exactly what my friend King Heiple did. King has generously shared the illustration on the facing page for his shop-built jig.

When I go out to do turning demonstrations, I only carry a Oneway Vari-Grind jig in my tool kit. On site I scrounge a board approximately

King Heiple's Shop-Built Jig

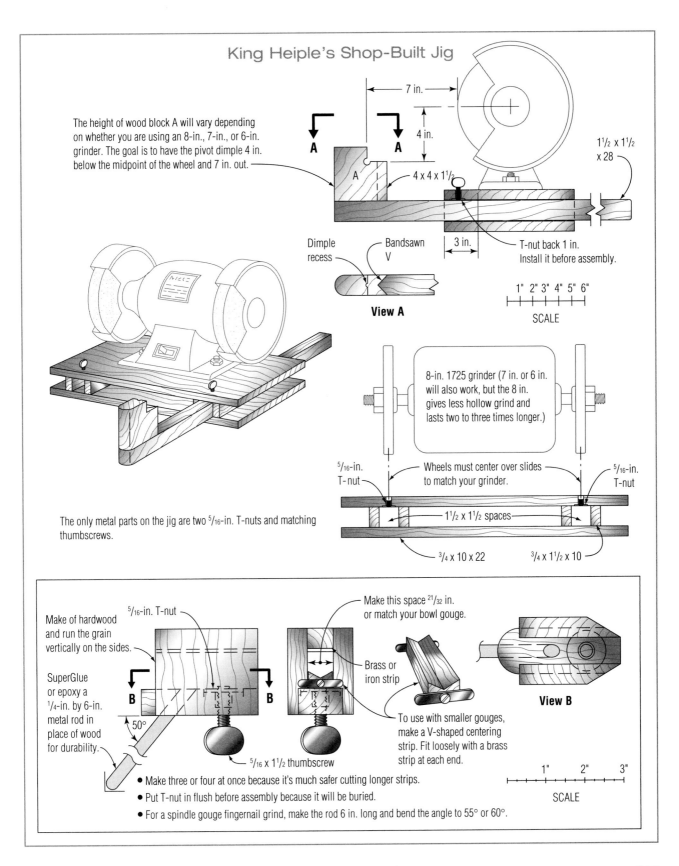

The height of wood block A will vary depending on whether you are using an 8-in., 7-in., or 6-in. grinder. The goal is to have the pivot dimple 4 in. below the midpoint of the wheel and 7 in. out.

7 in.

4 in.

A A

A

4 x 4 x 1½

$1½ x 1½$
x 28

Dimple recess

Bandsawn V

3 in.

T-nut back 1 in.
Install it before assembly.

View A

1" 2" 3" 4" 5" 6"

SCALE

8-in. 1725 grinder (7 in. or 6 in. will also work, but the 8 in. gives less hollow grind and lasts two to three times longer.)

The only metal parts on the jig are two $5/16$-in. T-nuts and matching thumbscrews.

$5/16$-in. T-nut

$5/16$-in. T-nut

Wheels must center over slides to match your grinder.

$1½ x 1½$ spaces

$3/4$ x 10 x 22

$3/4$ x 1½ x 10

Make of hardwood and run the grain vertically on the sides.

$5/16$-in. T-nut

Make this space $21/32$ in. or match your bowl gouge.

SuperGlue or epoxy a $1/4$-in. by 6-in. metal rod in place of wood for durability.

B B

50°

Brass or iron strip

To use with smaller gouges, make a V-shaped centering strip. Fit loosely with a brass strip at each end.

View B

$5/16$ x 1½ thumbscrew

- Make three or four at once because it's much safer cutting longer strips.
- Put T-nut in flush before assembly because it will be buried.
- For a spindle gouge fingernail grind, make the rod 6 in. long and bend the angle to 55° or 60°.

1" 2" 3"

SCALE

An economical approach is to buy Oneway's Vari-Grind jig and clamp a board with a dimple carved in it as a pocket for the leg of the jig.

¾ in. by 2 in. by 18 in. Using a spindle gouge, I carve a small dimple in one end of the board to accept the leg of the Vari-Grind jig. I then clamp this board under the grinder to form a quick and dirty pocket jig. Any woodworker could make a similar arm that adjusts easily and would only have to buy a Vari-Grind jig. Such an adjustable arm is shown in King Heiple's illustration.

Safety Equipment

Safety equipment is essential. It protects you from harm and makes turning a smoother operation. Without the following equipment, you risk injury.

PROTECTIVE CLOTHING
Always wear sturdy shoes when turning to provide protection against dropped tools or workpieces. Faceplate turners should wear safety shoes.

EYE PROTECTION
Some sort of eye protection is essential when operating a lathe. The minimum is a pair of shatterproof eyeglasses, preferably with side shields. For some types of work, such as turning wood with bark still on it or exceptionally splintery material, a full face shield should be worn. By law all prescription glasses sold in the United States are shatterproof and probably provide sufficient protection for many turning situations. However, most glasses have plastic lenses to save weight. The plastic attracts dust, and wiping it away dry (which is a necessity at times) scratches them quickly. I specify shatterproof glass lenses in safety frames when ordering my shop glasses. Though a bit heavy, they are much more scratch-resistant. Safety

frames also come with side shields, which are typically removable if you want a more casual look.

VENTILATION AND DUST COLLECTION

It is equally important to protect yourself from dust. Wood dust, especially from tropical species, can be quite toxic and even carcinogenic. A paper dust mask, like those worn in automotive body shops, is a minimum requirement. Better protection is afforded by a respirator, which has replaceable cartridge-type filters and looks like a military gas mask. Respirators offer good dust protection, but they're hot and tiring to wear because you're doing the air pumping with your lungs. They also are a problem for turners who have beards because of the difficulty in obtaining a tight seal.

The best form of protection for both the eyes and the lungs is an air helmet. Air helmets offer the safety of a full face shield and hard hat with excellent dust protection that does not tax your respiratory system. The helmet has a battery-powered motor that pumps air into it, which provides positive air pressure inside the shield, excluding dust and preventing fogging. Since the motor is doing the pumping instead of your lungs, breathing is much easier than with a respirator. Although some air helmets filter only dust, others also filter organic vapors from glues and finishing products. Air helmets cost a lot more than other types of dust protectors (as much as $750), but if you do much woodworking, they're well worth the price.

Lathe Safety Guidelines

- Make sure the lathe is properly grounded and meets local electric codes.
- Make sure the work is securely mounted in the lathe.
- Check for any defects in the wood you are planning to turn.
- Always start the lathe at an appropriate speed.
- Never touch or move the belt while the lathe is running, and never run the lathe without the belt cover in place.
- When mounting a new workpiece, check that the tool rest clears the work and that the rest is securely locked in position before starting the lathe.
- Listen for unusual sounds coming from the lathe. They can indicate that something is wrong.
- Always unplug the lathe while performing maintenance or repairs.
- Use the correct tools for the job. Roughing gouges and skew chisels should not be used for faceplate turning.
- Always work with tools that are sharp.
- Wear appropriate safety equipment for eye and lung protection, and wear clothes without dangling ends. Roll up your sleeves if you are wearing a long-sleeve shirt.
- Take frequent breaks, especially when doing repetitive work where your mind may drift.

Flyers and Speed

WORK FLYING OUT OF THE LATHE and glued-up work flying apart in the lathe constitute by far the biggest dangers in turning. In a few rare instances, flying work has even caused death—usually when the operator is hit in the head. Such accidents can almost always be traced back to starting the lathe at too high a speed for the turning operation.

You need to work out a routine that will prevent flyers. Form the habit of returning your lathe to its lowest speed at the end of every turning session. Unplugging it at this time and draping the plug across the bed is a great reminder. Make speed concerns the foremost thought in your mind as you approach the lathe, and make setting the appropriate speed the first order of business when chucking work. Rotate the work by hand to make sure that it clears the tool rest before you turn on the lathe. Finally, if you're the least unsure, stand to the left of the lathe when you turn it on. If the work is going to fly, you're out of the line of fire.

The tool rest provides some protection for the operator, since it directs a high percentage of flyers to the back of the lathe, but you also need to protect any observers in your shop. Flyers tend to travel at right angles to the headstock spindle, so don't let spectators stand in the area 90° to the spinning work. The best place for viewers to stand is around the tailstock. Warning others in the shop when you first start the lathe after mounting work will do much to prevent accidents.

Appropriate turning speed is a difficult thing to specify. As with driving a car, you can negotiate higher speeds as you gain experience, but for begin-

ners it's always best to err on the side of low speed. Except for miniature work, turning need never take place at a speed higher than 2,000 rpm. Sanding is best done at the final turning speed and does not, as some sources recommend, require higher speeds.

For turning spindles up to 2½ in. dia., a roughing speed of about 1,100 rpm and a finishing speed of about 1,700 rpm are appropriate. The experienced turner will be able to do the entire operation at the higher speed as long as the work is well centered to start.

Faceplate turning is more prone to flyers because of the greater diameter of the work and the greater difficulty in centering. For work up to 10 in. dia., 600 rpm to 800 rpm is a good roughing speed, and 1,100 rpm is an appropriate finishing speed. Facework need never be done at a speed greater than 1,100 rpm. For large-diameter facework, roughing speeds as low as 200 rpm may be necessary.

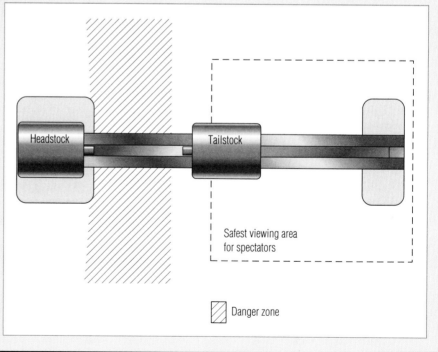

Headstock

Tailstock

Safest viewing area
for spectators

Danger zone

An air helmet offers the best all-around eye and dust protection to the turner. Ear protectors may also be added to this helmet for noisy situations.

Air-filtration systems that mount on the ceiling of your shop are also widely available. These units are simply air movers with filters to remove dust. The unit has to be sized to the cubic volume of your shop, and the filters have to be cleaned on a regular basis. Most filters can be cleaned with a shop vacuum numerous times before they need to be changed. Although air-filtration systems do not eliminate dust from the environment, they do minimize the exposure time and simplify cleanup. The best of all possible worlds is to have a filter and a helmet.

If your shop has a central dust-collection system, placing a pickup near your lathe can be useful for sucking up much of the dust from sanding. You will have to rig some sort of clamping system so that you can position the hose near the work. Dust collection will do little to suck up the chips (especially wet ones) created by the lathe until they are on the floor. Wet chips in the dust-collection bag or bin present a safety hazard due to spontaneous combustion, so bins should be emptied every session. Chips with oil finish present a similar hazard.

Air-filtration systems that continuously clean the air in your shop are a great second line of defense after a dust mask. They keep the shop cleaner as well. (Photo courtesy the JDS Company.)

Jigs for Special Techniques

There is the old joke that it only takes one woodworker to change a light bulb but that he has to build a jig to do it. So it is with the lathe. Woodworking literature is resplendent with myriad jigs for turning. Here is a small sampling.

POWER-SANDING

The easiest way to sand a bowl is with one of the many power-sanding systems that are on the market today. They get you through the drudgery of the coarse grits quickly. You can mount a sanding mandrel in a ¼-in. or ⅜-in. electric drill. You need a drill with lots of power and speed, so cordless drills are out. A corded, reversible drill that has a top speed of 1,500 rpm to 2,000 rpm is best—the faster the better! I call my sanding mandrel the electric skew.

I typically power-sand at the same speed at which I did the primary turning, although sometimes I even slow the lathe down. While it is tempting to speed up the lathe for sanding, that's dangerous and counter-productive. Faceplate work is often a bit out of round, which can happen as a green bowl dries in the lathe, and at high speed you will only sand the high spots. Power-sanding much beyond 120 grit with stock sanding systems does not work very well because the hard backing of the pad causes scratching. I hand-sand or modify my sanding system with a more resilient pad from 150 grit on up.

REEDING AND FLUTING WITH A ROUTER

Architecture and period furniture often have turnings with decorative elements such as flutes and reeds. Flutes and reeds can be thought of as coves and beads that run along the length of a spindle turning rather than around it. Flutes are concave grooves cut in the surface of the work, whereas reeds are convex beads raised on the surface.

The easiest way to sand most work in the lathe is with a power-sanding mandrel mounted in an electric drill. On the left is a Snap-loc system made by Merrit Abrasives. Each sanding disk has a small plastic clutch that snaps into the rubber mandrel. On the right is a home-made mandrel that accepts Klingspor hooks and loops to hold the abrasives.

Turning Your Lathe into a Drill Press

IF YOU WANT TO MAKE YOUR LATHE into a drill press, you can fit a drill pad—in effect, a mini drill-press table—into the tailstock spindle. Years ago, drill pads were a common accessory for both metal and wood lathes, but now you'll probably have to make your own since they're hard to find. The illustration below shows a plan for a drill pad that will fit a #2 Morse-taper spindle. For strength, the pad is best made in two pieces, using a hardwood such as maple or red oak. The Morse taper is spindle-turned, while the pad is faceplate-turned.

Place a drill of the appropriate diameter in the headstock, and hold the work on the drill pad. Use the tailstock handwheel to advance the table and work into the drill. As in drilling with a drill press, make sure you can hold the work with sufficient leverage to keep it from spinning. The bigger the drill, the more leverage you'll require.

Drill Pad

$^9/_{16}$ in.

$^9/_{16}$ in. dia.

$2^{11}/_{16}$ in.

$^{11}/_{16}$ in. dia.

3 in. dia.

The best way to make the drill pad is to turn a taper separately with a tenon on the end. Make the pad out of $^1/_2$-in. or $^3/_4$-in. plywood, drill to tenon size, and glue together.

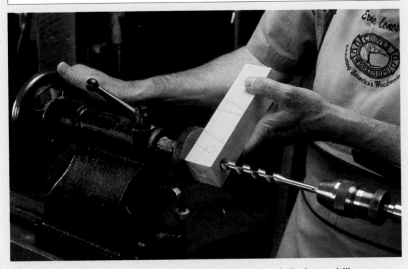

A drill pad is a nifty shopmade accessory that will turn you lathe into a drill press.

The Power Skew

A power-sanding mandrel is also good for long, straight spindle work, such as columns and table legs. I call it the power skew.

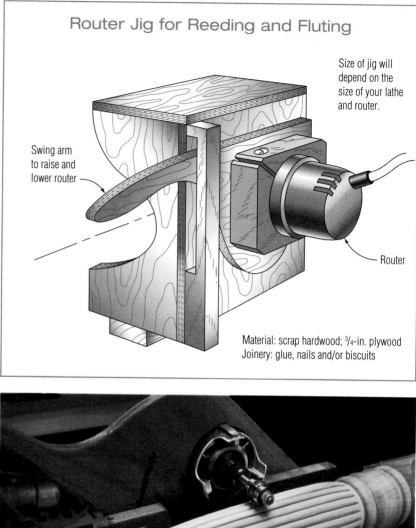

Router Jig for Reeding and Fluting

Size of jig will depend on the size of your lathe and router.

Swing arm to raise and lower router

Router

Material: scrap hardwood; ³/₄-in. plywood
Joinery: glue, nails and/or biscuits

In combination with the lathe's indexing system, this shop-built jig will mill reeds and flutes.

Because flutes and reeds run along the axis of the work, they can't be turned, but they can be made in the lathe while the machine is not running. This type of work can be accomplished by employing a router in a jig in conjunction with the lathe's indexing mechanism. There are many jigs for cutting flutes and reeds that work well. The illustration above shows a simple router jig that you can build.

CUTTING DOVETAILS IN COLUMN BASES WITH A ROUTER

Columns for Philadelphia pie-crust tables, tea tables, and similar structures typically have three legs (often cabriole) attached at the bottom of the column. Attaching the feet is best done with a dovetail joint. Dovetail slots are made in the base of the column, and matching dovetails are cut in the legs so that they may be attached by sliding in from the bottom of the column.

Historically, dovetails were cut with a backsaw and chiseled out in much the same way that a half-blind dovetail is cut by hand. Today, it is better done with a router in the lathe.

It is simple to build a suitable jig for making the cuts (see the illustration below). The jig is essentially a box that surrounds the work and has a wood key on the bottom that matches the gap in the lathe bed. A slot in the top of the jig matches a guide bushing on the router. I use a large carbide-tipped dovetail bit to mill the dovetail. You can make the matching dovetail on the leg on a router table with the same dovetail bit. Using the router table, I hold the work with a tenoning jig from my table saw. I run the tenoning jig in the router table's miter slot.

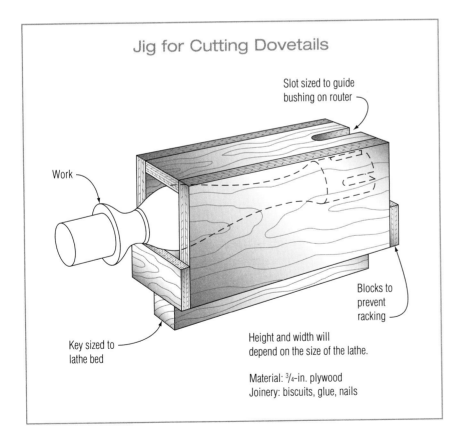

Jig for Cutting Dovetails

Slot sized to guide bushing on router

Work

Blocks to prevent racking

Key sized to lathe bed

Height and width will depend on the size of the lathe.

Material: 3/4-in. plywood
Joinery: biscuits, glue, nails

Here is a spiral column and a two-flute closed spiral of a tighter twist.

MULTIPLE STARTS FOR SPIRAL TURNING

Number of starts	Pitch range
One	1 to 1¼ times the diameter of the turning
Two	2 times the diameter of the turning
Three	2½ to 3 times the diameter of the turning
Four	2 times the diameter of the turning

SPIRAL TURNING

Spiral turning has been around for centuries. Furniture and homes of the 18th and even 17th centuries are full of spiral turnings. I typically elect to do this job by hand because I never have had to make more than two, but there are new tools and jigs that make cutting spirals easier than ever.

One such tool is the Sorby spiral tool, which has a serrated wheel at the end of a shaft that is mounted in a base plate. The shaft can be rotated in the base plate but locks at the desired amount of rotation via socket head screws. The more the rotation left or right, the steeper the pitch of the spirals generated. The base plate contacts the tool rest and keeps the entire tool at the same angle throughout the cut.

The tool is presented in a downhill scrape cut. The wheel revolves during the cut, which at first is a bit unnerving. Once the cut starts, you should keep the tool in contact with the work and slowly advance left or right (depending on the direction of the spiral). You then withdraw the tool and return to the start point. The wheel will pick up the first cut, and you move the tool in again as before. Lathe speeds should be kept moderate.

This open, double-barley twist candlestick took me about six hours to make, but much of the time was spent in carefully sanding the twists and applying repeated coats of oil finish.

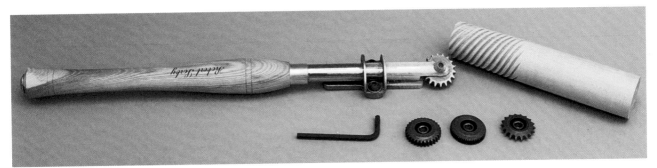

Sorby spiralling tools will cut multistart twists in spindles. The pitch of the spiral is controlled by how far the wheel is angled to the right or left.

If you do the job by hand, you need to get the layout right. The top of a single thread is referred to as the crest, while the valley between two adjacent threads is referred to as the root. Normally, ornamental spirals are rather steep in pitch. While pitch in screw threads is generally thought of as the number of turns of thread per inch (measured between crests), in spiral woodturning the pitch is set by the diameter of the work. If you had a 2-in.-dia. cylinder, for example, one pitch would be one turn in 2 in.

In most cases, spiral turnings entail multiple starts so that you have two, three, four, or more threads starting at evenly spaced intervals around the turning. The more starts you employ, the steeper the pitch must become to make the turning look right. By drilling through the center of a multiple-start turning, the twist can be made "open," which is very attractive. For twists that have a bit of taper, the pitch is the diameter at the thickest spot, which is usually at or near the base. The chart on the facing page gives you a good starting point for laying out various twist patterns.

If you want to produce spiral turnings on a production basis, you should look into the line of Legacy Ornamental Milling Systems made by Phantom Engineering. Ranging in price from $750 to $3,500, they turn out spirals in a hurry.

ORNAMENTAL TURNING

Although ornamental turning (OT) enjoyed a strong following in the 19th century, it was a province only of the wealthy. Happily, the hobby is within the means of almost anyone today. The cost is reasonable because you can buy attachments that add ornamental capability to a normal woodturning lathe.

Woodcraft sells a nice ornamental attachment that fits the Jet mini lathe. Designed by Jerry Beal, it works beautifully but can only do small work. Although it is intended for pens, it can handle anything within the capacity of the Jet lathe. It is strongest in side-cutting mode, where it will mill spirals as well as simple geometric patterns. End-grain cutting is under development at the time of this writing. The basic Beal attachment sells for about $350, but it also requires a Fordem shaft tool, which raises the cost to about $550.

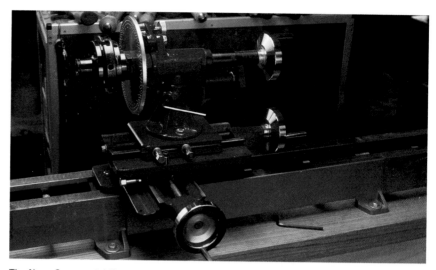

The Nova Ornamental Turner adds ornamental turning capabilities to any lathe with 8 in. or more center height. Teknatool also has a 7-in. model with adapter kits for many lathes.

The most ambitious OT attachment is the Nova Ornamental Turner. Although the Nova attachment is designed for the Nova 3000 lathe, it can be retrofitted to almost any lathe with 8 in. or greater center height— even my wood-bed lathe. Nova also has a model for lathes with up to 7 in. center height (14-in. swing), and it is developing adapter kits for popular lathe brands and models. The attachment costs about $550.

The Nova Ornamental Turner is essentially a saddle (like those found on metal lathes) with a spindle unit mounted on the top. The saddle is composed of two slides that travel in x- and y-axes. The cross slide travels in the y-axis (90° to the lathe bed), while the compound slide is typically run in the x-axis (parallel to the lathe bed). The compound slide can, however, be adjusted to any angle for cutting tapers and special operations. Both the cross slide and the compound slide have stops that can be set to limit travel so as to make every cut of equal depth.

The saddle replaces the tailstock of the lathe during OT operations. The spindle unit in essence is identical to the headstock spindle with the same thread (1¼ in. x 8) and #2 MT. (There is a 1-in. x 8 thread on the 7-in. model.) The two spindles oppose each other. Work that has been turned on a faceplate or in a chuck can be transferred to the spindle unit and brought into play with a variety of cutters that are mounted on the headstock spindle. The spindle unit actually mounts in a pedestal base, which in turn mounts on the top of the compound. A grub screw in the side of the pedestal locks the height and alignment of the spindle unit.

The Nova Ornamental Turner allows four types of ornamental work: end-grain cutting, side cutting, threading, and metalturning.

End-grain cutting If you recall the child's toy called a spirograph, then you'll easily understand ornamental end-grain cutting. The spirograph created geometric designs on paper by changing gears and the length of the arms holding the pen. For ornamental end-grain cutting, a bit is placed in the cutter frame, which is mounted on the headstock spindle. A screw adjustment in the cutter frame allows placing the bit any distance from the center so as to circumscribe a circle. The work is attached via a faceplate or chuck to the spindle unit and brought into play with the cutter via the compound slide. Cuts are made at regular intervals around the work with the aid of the indexing plate so as to create geometric patterns (see the photos below). The indexing plate has three circles of holes—96 holes, 72 holes, and 24 holes—which allow just about any spacing imaginable.

This screw-thread box (open) has a barleycorn pattern on the lid and side cutting on the lid and base.

This is a traditional barleycorn pattern that is made by cutting five consecutive holes in the 96-hole dividing plate, then skipping three holes.

Grub Screw Problems

As the grub screw bites into the mounting shaft of the spindle unit, fine nuances of adjustment become impossible. I cure this problem by placing a slug of brass under the grub screw. I recommend doing this whenever you set up the unit.

Side cutting allows the milling of geometric patterns into the side of a turning.

Side cutting In side cutting, the cross slide is used to bring the edge of the work into play with a cutter mounted on a boring bar, which in turn is threaded on the headstock spindle (see the photo above). The indexing plate is used to make the cuts at regular intervals around the periphery of the work so as to create interesting texture and patterns. It is easy to over-do side cutting and wind up with a busy result. Simplicity is usually better.

Threading Threading is one of the neatest capabilities of the Nova Ornamental Turner. It allows you to make boxes with screw-on lids as well as a variety of threaded parts of 1 in. dia. or greater. For threading, one of three threading bushes is placed on the spindle unit and a half-nut is engaged into the bush. Turning the handwheel on the spindle unit advances the spindle at the pitch of the bush. A 60° cutter is placed in the boring bar, and the work is brought into contact with the cutter via the cross slide. Once in contact with the cutter, the work is advanced along the axis of the lathe via the handwheel on the spindle unit. It is imperative that the compound slide is not moved after the initial cut, or the thread will be ruined. Both internal and external threads may be milled with results in wood far superior to chasing.

The thread pitches of the bushes are metric. In the metric system, pitch is measured by the distance between two adjacent crests rather than the number of crests in 1 in. The bushes are 1.5mm (about 17 pitch), 2mm (about 12½ pitch), and 3mm (about 8½ pitch). One could only wish that the third bush was 8 pitch exactly because then you could mill 1¼ in. x 8 threads, which is the size of the headstock spindle on the Nova 3000. I made such a bush for my Nova Ornamental Turner, but not everyone has a metalturning lathe to perform this task.

Virtual End-Grain Cutting

You can purchase an end-grain cutting program for your computer called the Ornamental Turning Companion. With this software, you can visualize placement and cutting patterns to save you wood, time, and money. Even without an OT attachment, you can do some virtual end-grain cutting.

The Nova Ornamental Turner attachment enables you to cut screw threads in wood.

Three different threading bushes, which mount on the spindle unit, allow you to mill a host of useful threads. The one on the spindle is 2mm, which is about 12½ pitch.

Metalturning By replacing the spindle unit with a tool holder, you get a metalturning lathe. You can cut cylinders or tapers with a compound slide and perform face cuts with a cross slide. You can, of course, also cut wood to a high degree of accuracy, which could be useful for pattern-makers. The only additional thing you could want is travel dials on the handwheel of the two slides to track travel in thousandths of an inch. Remember that when advancing the cross slide, you take double the advance off of the work because you are cutting both sides. Therefore, an advance of .015 in. actually reduces the diameter by 1/16 in.

Lathe Duplicators

While it's my firm belief that lathe duplicators have no place in a small shop, I concede that they can save a considerable amount of time on large-scale production jobs. A duplicator is an auxiliary carriage that's bolted onto a lathe bed with a knife connected to a pantograph that travels freely on the carriage. A master part is placed between centers in the duplicator, which is normally at the front of the lathe. A billet of the appropriate diameter is placed between the actual centers of the lathe, then the panto-graph traces the master and moves the knife proportionally. Although some duplicators have sophisticated knives that cut tangentially, others make a simple scrape cut—the kind of cut I have been telling you to avoid. Finally, a decent duplicator is going to cost $2,000 or more these days, and cheaper ones are not worth having.

6

Tools

When it comes to tools, the good news is that a vast selection is offered in the marketplace. Unfortunately, there are some really bad tools in addition to some really good ones. Compounding the problem, most turning tools are not delivered properly shaped or sharpened and need a good deal of user tuning (grinding to the correct shape) and honing to work properly (see chapter 5 for information on grinders and sharpening jigs).

Most aspiring turners try to use tools directly from the package, doing nothing more than honing to a sharp edge. They are disappointed by the results and blame themselves when things do not go well. The fact is that most people take to turning like ducks to water if sharp tools of the correct shapes are placed in their hands. If you follow my prescriptions for tool shapes and sharpening in this chapter, you will find learning to turn an easier process.

Turning tools are available in three materials: high-carbon steel, high-speed steel (HSS), and powdered metal technology steel (PMTS). Traditionally, turning tools were made out of high-carbon steel, which is iron with ¾ percent to 1½ percent carbon as the principal alloying element. Such steel is often referred to as "water-hardening" steel because it must be quenched in water during hardening.

Water-hardening steel tools are still widely available, but in the last two decades manufacturers have increasingly switched to high-speed steel for their premium turning-tool lines. HSS tools are more expensive, but they hold an edge substantially longer, thus requiring less frequent sharpening. HSS also has the quality of "hot hardness." Whereas carbon steel cannot be heated higher than 430°F without drawing the temper, HSS maintains its hardness at much higher temperatures and is thus more immune to damage from burning and overheating due to excessive grinding. HSS is more expensive because tungsten, cobalt, and molybdenum must be alloyed into the steel in addition to carbon.

Another desirable alloying element is vanadium, which forms vanadium carbide in the steel structure. Vanadium carbide is highly wear-resistant, which makes for better edge holding. In conventional steel making, alloying elements in the right proportions are mixed while molten and poured into a mold to form an ingot. The problem is that during cooling, vanadium carbide "freezes out" first, creating areas of greater and lesser concentrations of the vanadium carbide. At vanadium levels much above a 4 percent, "stringers" are created in the resulting ingot that are so hard that they make the steel difficult to machine or grind.

PMTS can have vanadium levels as high as 15 percent. This type of steel is created by spraying a powdered mixture of the desired proportions through a nozzle into an inert-atmosphere furnace where tiny spheres of metal are formed. The resulting powdered metal is then rolled into sheets and bars by using conventional cold working processes. The alloys of the original molten mixture become evenly distributed through the PMTS, giving it a homogenous structure that is free of stringers.

Tool Hardness

THE HARDNESS OF TOOL STEEL is measured in the Rockwell C Scale, which measures the penetration of a specially shaped diamond into the material under a specific load. Readings are expressed as Hardness Rockwell C (HRC). Under the C Scale, a diamond would measure 100 HRC and a metal file would measure about 64 HRC. As it arrives from the mill, steel is about 30 HRC, but all turning tools need to be much harder than this to hold an edge.

To harden the steel, it's put through a heat-treating process. The first stage is hardening. Freshly forged high-carbon tool steel is heated to cherry red then quenched in water. This leaves the steel at full hardness, around 64 HRC. The hardness is then tempered in a process called drawing. The steel is heated to a predetermined temperature, which draws back the hardness to the desired level, typically 58 HRC to 60 HRC for gouges and chisels. Without drawing, the steel would be too brittle; the drawing process actually toughens the tools.

High-speed steels have properties (imparted by the alloying of tungsten and molybdenum) that make them more difficult to heat-treat but on the other hand more difficult to damage due to overheating during grinding or use. Heat-treating of HSS requires heating to much higher temperatures during the hardening process. Instead of being quenched in water, it can be quenched in moving air. The oxide formed on the surface in air would be unacceptable, however, so heat-treating is actually done in a vacuum or in inert gas atmosphere furnaces.

PMTS is expensive and much more difficult to machine. However, turning tools made from such metal hold their edges a long time. Some kinds of PMTS are not high-speed steels, so they should be given the same care to prevent overheating during grinding as carbon-steel tools. Many PMTS are HSS, though, and in fact the best high-speed steels are now made by powdered metal technology. Examples are M-4, M-42, and T15. When purchasing PMTS tools, it is best to check the manufacturer's instructions as to grinding temperatures. There are a few small manufacturers (such as Jerry Glaser Engineering Company) making tools from PMTS.

If you're one of the lucky few for whom money is no object, I recommend that you buy only HSS or PMTS turning tools. If, like most of us, you have to watch your budget, begin with high-carbon steel tools or a mix of carbon steel, HSS, and PMTS tools, then upgrade as your budget permits. Remember that generations of turners have produced wonderful results without the benefit of HSS or PMTS. With carbon-steel tools (and some PMTS), you just have to be more careful not to overheat the metal during grinding. By using a grinding jig (see pp. 92–98), this is a simple matter nowadays.

Premium tools are offered in two types: standard and long-and-strong. Standard tools are for spindle work, while the more robust long-and-strong tools are for heavy-duty faceplate work. You would only need long-and-strong tools if you progress to turning large bowls.

When buying tools, avoid commercial sets, unless they are such bargains that you cannot pass them up. Sets tend to include only two or three tools you really need, while the rest eventually become expensive scrapers.

Throughout this chapter, I will speak of short, medium, and long bevels to describe grinding angles (see the illustration on the facing page). This age-old way of describing grind angles is an excellent one for comparing two identical tools. A thick tool with a short bevel can be confused with a thin tool with a long bevel, however. To avoid this confusion, the

---

Is It HSS?

Do a spark test on your tool before you grind it the first time to see if it's HSS. If you get a white starburst, it's not an HSS tool and should not be overheated in a grinder. If you get an orange ball that looks like a meteor, you have HSS.

Tools to Start

IF YOU'RE JUST STARTING OUT, you may be confused about what tool to buy first. I would build a set of HSS or PMTS tools in the following order:

- ½-in. spindle gouge
- ½-in. or ⅜-in. bowl gouge
- ¾-in. to 1¼-in. roughing-out gouge
- 1-in. or larger skew chisel
- ⅛-in. parting tool
- scrapers

If possible buy HSS or PMTS tools. However, you can get by with a carbon-steel skew chisel since, barring calamity (i.e., an edge-first fall onto a concrete floor), it can be sharpened exclusively on stones. Similarly, you can easily make scrapers from any available piece of steel.

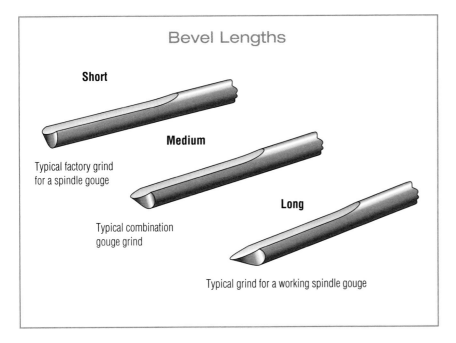

Bevel Lengths

Short

Typical factory grind
for a spindle gouge

Medium

Typical combination
gouge grind

Long

Typical grind for a working spindle gouge

GRINDING ANGLES FOR VARIOUS BEVEL LENGTHS

Bevel length	Grind angle
Short	65° to 85° (typically about 75°)
Medium	About 45°
Long	25° to 30°

chart above connects bevel length to inclusive angles of grind. In general, scrapers are ground to short bevels, but the resulting burr is what does the cutting. Faceplate tools are generally ground to medium bevels and spindle tools to long bevels.

Gouges

The most basic turning tool is a gouge. It is a stalwart friend in either spindle or faceplate work. If I were banished to a desert island with a lathe and just one tool, I would pick a spindle gouge. Mastery of the spindle gouge is mastery of turning itself.

Traditionally, gouges were forged, and many are still made that way. Forging entails heating the steel in a forge and hammering it while hot to the correct shape. At one time, a local blacksmith or even the turner himself did the forging, but since the Industrial Revolution, it has mostly been done in drop forges. Drop-forging mechanizes the hand-forging process by replacing the blacksmith's anvil and hammer with a set of dies of the correct shapes. The dies are put in a powerful press that repeatedly closes

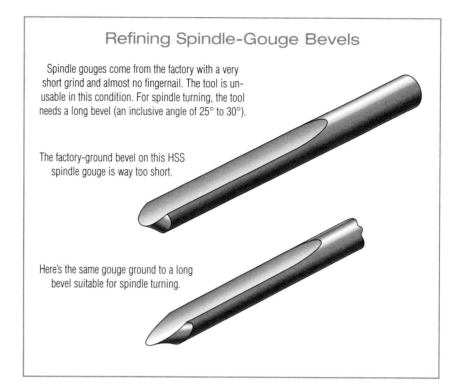

Refining Spindle-Gouge Bevels

Spindle gouges come from the factory with a very short grind and almost no fingernail. The tool is unusable in this condition. For spindle turning, the tool needs a long bevel (an inclusive angle of 25° to 30°).

The factory-ground bevel on this HSS spindle gouge is way too short.

Here's the same gouge ground to a long bevel suitable for spindle turning.

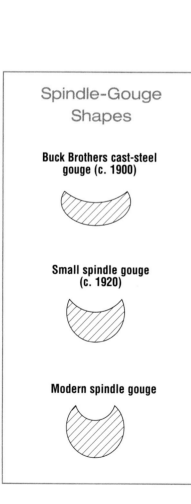

Spindle-Gouge Shapes

Buck Brothers cast-steel gouge (c. 1900)

Small spindle gouge (c. 1920)

Modern spindle gouge

them around the heated metal. The result is highly consistent, with one gouge looking like the next. Forged turning tools are made of carbon steel, the most basic form of tool steel.

Because of the advantages of alloy steels, manufacturers of premium tools now turn HSS and PMTS. The problem is that most HSS and PMTS do not forge well, so gouges made from these materials are typically machined from bar stock. Although this gives modern gouges a somewhat different look and feel from tools of the past, in reality the shape of a good modern gouge is very similar to a good traditional gouge. The problem is that not all gouges are created equal, and *none* come ground to a usable shape, let alone sharp.

SPINDLE GOUGES

Traditionally, spindle gouges were made of heavy section with the bottom half being nearly a semicircle (see the illustration at left). They behaved much like a modern HSS gouge machined from round bar stock. After World War II, large retailers, such as Sears and Montgomery Ward, started offering inexpensive lines of turning tools (mostly in sets) for hobbyists. The cheaper prices were achieved by using shorter and thinner blanks of steel and shorter handles. Persisting to this day, these tools are flat in cross section, so flat that they neither roll beads nor cut deep coves well.

In my opinion, a gouge that is round in section (at least the bottom half) is the easiest for most people to use. You can achieve a better-shaped fingernail on a rounded section (see the illustration above), which more readily conforms to the shapes of coves and beads. The shape also gives the tool more stability because it puts the area of contact with the tool rest under the center of the force where the cutting takes place. With flatter tools that have an oval section, contact with the rest can be to one side of the area where the cut is taking place.

The best spindle gouges have flutes that are a radius and not too deep. This shape achieves a long fingernail yet keeps the area that is cutting over the point where the shank contacts the rest.

Sharpening a Spindle Gouge

A simple bar-type rest is the best for sharpening spindle gouges freehand.

1 Touch at the nose and immediately start swinging the tool either to the right or to the left. In this case, I am swinging to the right.

2 As you swing the tool, you must simultaneously tip the tool upward (the handle down) and rotate the handle slightly. Rotate the handle clockwise if swinging to the right and counterclockwise if swinging to the left.

3 Repeat the same steps in mirror image for the other half of the tool.

In the past, many people have tried to use what I call a pocket jig to grind a spindle gouge. The handle is pocketed in a cup on a sliding arm in front of the grinder and simply rotated against the wheel (see the illustration below). The problem with this arrangement is that although the point is ground fine, the sides of the fingernail lack clearance, with the edge being inside the bevel.

The Oneway, Sorby, and Tormek jigs improve on ordinary pocket jigs by fixing the tool in an adjustable gooseneck, which itself rests in a pocket. The result is a perfect fingernail grind with correct side angles. The angle of the gooseneck and the actual length of the bevel control the relationship between the point and sides of the fingernail. Angle of grind is controlled by how far the pocket is placed from the grinding wheel. On the Oneway jig, the pocket is on an arm that slides in and out just below the wheel. On the Sorby, the same result is achieved by adjusting the length of the gooseneck, and on the Tormek, the mounting arm for the gooseneck can be raised and lowered.

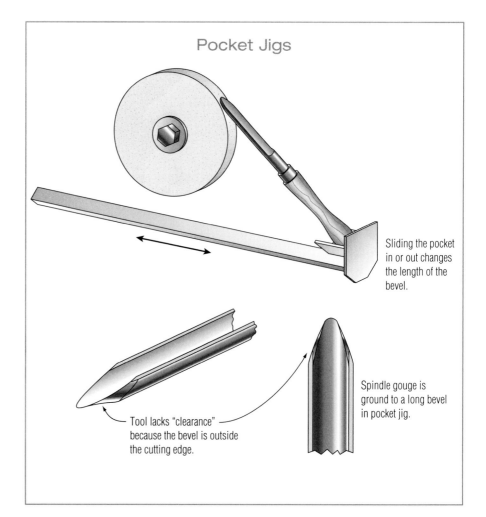

Pocket Jigs

Sliding the pocket in or out changes the length of the bevel.

Tool lacks "clearance" because the bevel is outside the cutting edge.

Spindle gouge is ground to a long bevel in pocket jig.

A roughing-out gouge may be sharpened on a platform rest (left) or in a pocket jig (right). The platform rest is better because tool-handle length precludes a long bevel on most home-shop-sized grinders.

ROUGHING-OUT GOUGES

The roughing-out gouge is a useful tool. It can remove large amounts of material quickly and is great for rounding billets fast. I also find it useful for cutting cylinders and tapers. If ground to a long bevel, it produces results nearly as good as a skew does with none of the behavior problems associated with skews. Most large spindle gouges make good roughing-out gouges, which is a good way to use a less-than-adequate spindle gouge if you're on a budget.

In the past, American turners left a bit of a fingernail on roughing-out gouges, which meant they could be used to cut large coves since they were just large forged gouges. Today, most turners follow the English tradition of grinding them square. Whichever way you grind them is largely a matter of taste and training. Both grinds work equally well. I prefer a square British grind because it is easier to do.

To sharpen a roughing-out gouge, you can use either a platform rest or a pocket jig. I generally employ a platform rest because I get more consistency from gouge to gouge. The long handle length of some modern HSS examples means you can't obtain a long bevel with a pocket jig. For those who are good at freehand grinding, you can simply plant your feet well in front of the grinder and rest the tool handle on your thigh. Your leg acts as a pocket jig (see the photo at right).

Today, HSS roughing-out gouges tend to be made from ⅛-in. HSS flat stock, which is cut to a basic outline, then hot-bent to form a U. Although the factory grind for the HSS variety has a cutting edge (or face) that is square to the shank of the tool and a medium bevel, the tool works much better with a long bevel about 25° to 30° (see the illustration on p. 120). For HSS roughing-out gouges, bigger is better—I like the 1¼-in. size.

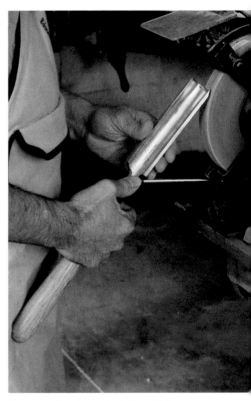

If you are already comfortable with free-hand grinding, you don't need a jig or a rest. Simply plant your feet well in front of the grinder, and rest the tool handle on your thigh.

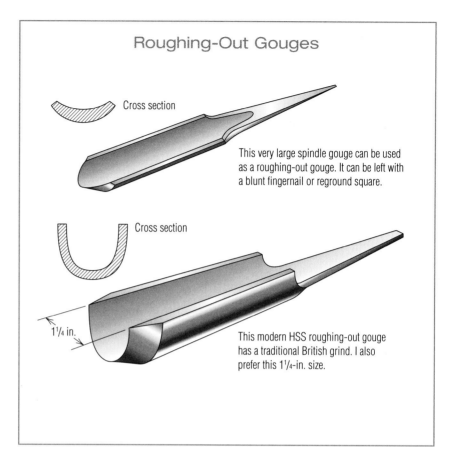

Roughing-Out Gouges

Cross section

This very large spindle gouge can be used as a roughing-out gouge. It can be left with a blunt fingernail or reground square.

Cross section

1¼ in.

This modern HSS roughing-out gouge has a traditional British grind. I also prefer this 1¼-in. size.

BOWL GOUGES

The bowl gouge is designed for faceplate turning, in which the grain of the wood runs across the axis of the lathe. The long bevel of a spindle gouge would readily dig into the reverse grain, causing a nasty catch. The bowl gouge provides a two-fold solution: Shorten the bevel of the gouge (the traditional angle is 45°), and cut at right angles to the axes of rotation. In this cutting position, the bottom half of the flute does all of the work and the nose bevel rides on the cylinder (or cone) being generated by the cut. This prevents the gouge from following the reverse grain and gives you a nice cut.

Bowl gouges have much deeper flutes than spindle gouges. Traditionally, they were forged with deep U-shaped bevels, which is ground all the way around to 45° (see the illustration on the facing page). The face is square to the shank. In fact, it is ground much like a roughing-out gouge, except that the bevel is shorter. Modern bowl gouges, machined from HSS round bar stock, generally have parabolic-shaped flutes.

Most turners find the tool more useful if they modify the factory grind. The simplest modification is to rake the face of the tool back at least 15° but retain the 45° bevel (see the photos on p. 122). You can further modify

Bowl-Gouge Grind

A modified factory grind is the best grind for learning to use a bowl gouge.

Bowl-Gouge Profiles

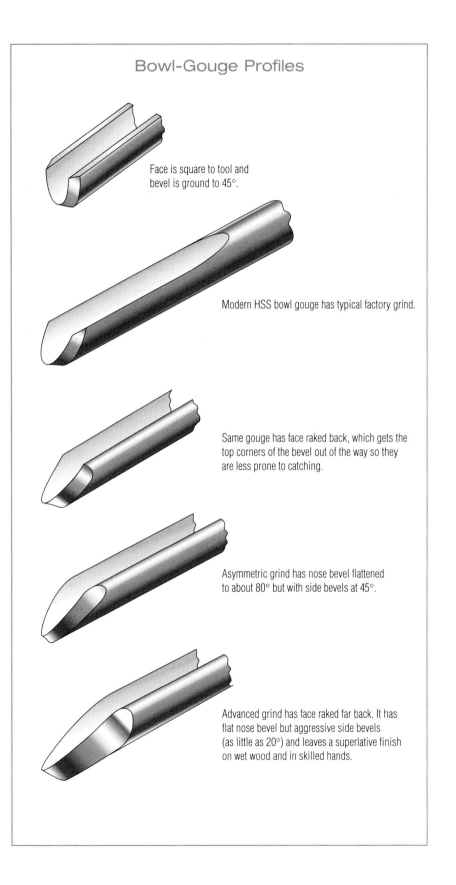

Face is square to tool and bevel is ground to 45°.

Modern HSS bowl gouge has typical factory grind.

Same gouge has face raked back, which gets the top corners of the bevel out of the way so they are less prone to catching.

Asymmetric grind has nose bevel flattened to about 80° but with side bevels at 45°.

Advanced grind has face raked far back. It has flat nose bevel but aggressive side bevels (as little as 20°) and leaves a superlative finish on wet wood and in skilled hands.

it by going to an asymmetric grind whereby the nose bevel is flattened in relation to the side bevels, which remain at 45°. This grind is much better for turning the insides of deep bowls because the nose bevel does not lose contact when it goes around the area between the side wall and the bottom. A 45° nose bevel loses contact at this area, resulting in a rough cut.

Many bowl turners grind the side bevels back further and increase the length of the bevel at the sides. In skilled hands, this grind can cut through reverse grain with hardly any tearout, but it negates much of the forgiving nature of a bowl gouge. Instead of rolling out of trouble, the gouge tends to dig in deeper. I urge you to become proficient with one of the milder grinds before progressing to this one.

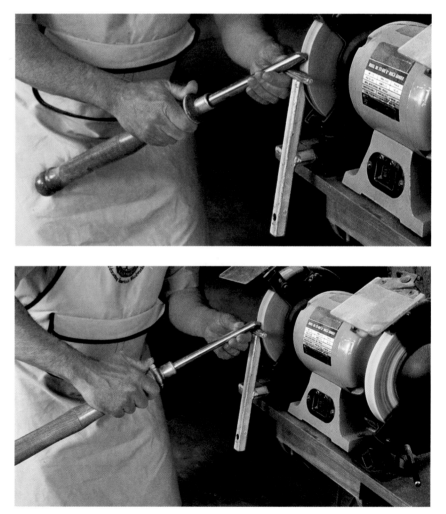

To achieve a general-purpose grind on a bowl gouge, start by touching one side of the bevel to the wheel to grind an approximately 45° angle. (The entire cutting edge, on that half of the flute, should be fairly square to the wheel.) Here I am starting with the left flank. Next, swing the handle toward center while simultaneously raising and twisting it. Repeat the process in mirror image for the other half of the tool.

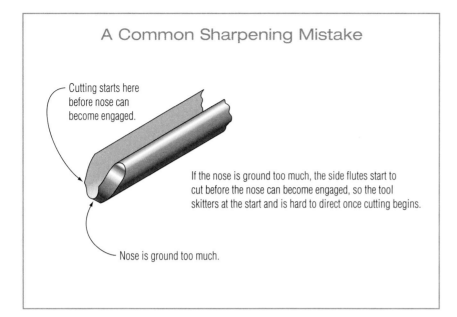

A Common Sharpening Mistake

Cutting starts here before nose can become engaged.

If the nose is ground too much, the side flutes start to cut before the nose can become engaged, so the tool skitters at the start and is hard to direct once cutting begins.

Nose is ground too much.

It is easy to grind more at the nose than on the side bevels, resulting in the shape shown in the illustration above. This shape makes the tool hard to start because the protruding side bevel will begin cutting before the nose has a chance to engage itself on the cut. Because the nose is small in relation to the side bevels, it will be ground away quicker than the sides if you don't grind lightly in the nose area. With a properly ground bevel, the nose engages simultaneously with the start of the lower bevel's cut. I use a bowl gouge straight from the grinder without buffing it.

COMBINATION GOUGES

In the last decade, rather long HSS gouges with medium flutes have emerged (see the top illustration on p. 124). These combination gouges can be ground to a medium bevel angle to do either faceplate or spindle work. In truth, they do not work in spindle turning as well as a true spindle gouge (see the bottom illustration on p. 116). They cannot be ground to the really long bevel necessary for top-quality spindle work. This is because a 30° bevel breaks through at the sides of the flute too low, leaving a ragged burr at the flanks.

The best use of a combination gouge is for taking a final light cut in faceplate work. You should present the tool much like a bowl gouge but more uphill. The tool can cut to the left or right, with the bevel riding behind the cut to prevent the tool from digging into the reverse grain areas. Used lightly, a combination gouge can save hours of sanding.

You can sharpen this gouge by eye in much the same way as a spindle gouge, but I recommend sharpening this tool in a jig. I buff a combination gouge to achieve a really keen edge.

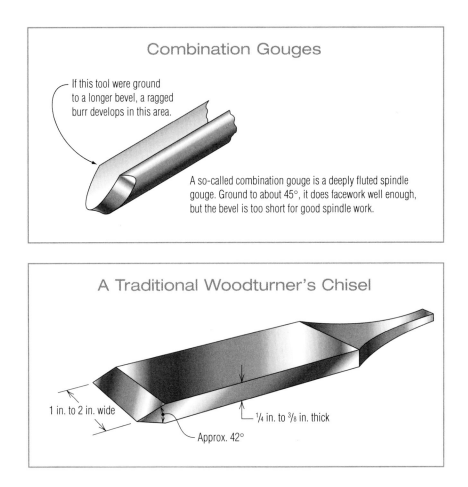

Combination Gouges

If this tool were ground to a longer bevel, a ragged burr develops in this area.

A so-called combination gouge is a deeply fluted spindle gouge. Ground to about 45°, it does facework well enough, but the bevel is too short for good spindle work.

A Traditional Woodturner's Chisel

1 in. to 2 in. wide

¼ in. to ⅜ in. thick

Approx. 42°

Chisels

I'll now turn my attention to the second family of turning tools—chisels. Unlike a woodworker's chisel, which is single beveled, a turner's chisel is double beveled. The edge is in the center of the blank with a bevel extending to either side (see the bottom illustration above). Although difficult to find, it is still possible to buy a traditional turner's chisel. A typical chisel is 1 in. to 2 in. wide, about 20 in. long (including the stout handle), and ground with the edge square to the blank (like a woodworker's chisel) with double flat bevels that meet at approximately a 42° inclusive angle. The chisel is the one tool in a turner's repertoire that works better with a flat rather than hollow-ground bevel.

You should present a traditional woodturner's chisel to the wood as shown in the illustration on the facing page. Since the illustration depicts cutting to the left, the chisel is turned slightly toward that direction and only the edge of the tool contacts the rest. A common beginner's mistake is to try to lay the entire tool flat on the rest before presenting it to the work.

I like to lock my fingers around the right edge of a chisel using a relaxed but firm grip. The real control of this tool comes from twisting it ever so slightly up and down to keep it cutting correctly. A beginner often makes the mistake of trying to raise and lower the handle or swing the handle left and right to control the cut. In the split second the cut gets the least off of the bevel, the edge starts cutting a helix in the work and is drawn down toward the rest with the corner (T) digging in. These catches

How a Chisel Cuts

The bevel we cannot see (the one on the far side of the tool) is rubbing the work and the edge is cutting somewhere between the dotted lines "A" and "B". The cut should take place in an area to the left of center of the tool (as shown by the shaded area), and no more than half the length of the cutting edge should be engaged. This puts the cut in an area just to the right of the corner of the chisel "H" and somewhere just to the right of center. The other corner of the chisel "T" is well clear of the cut.

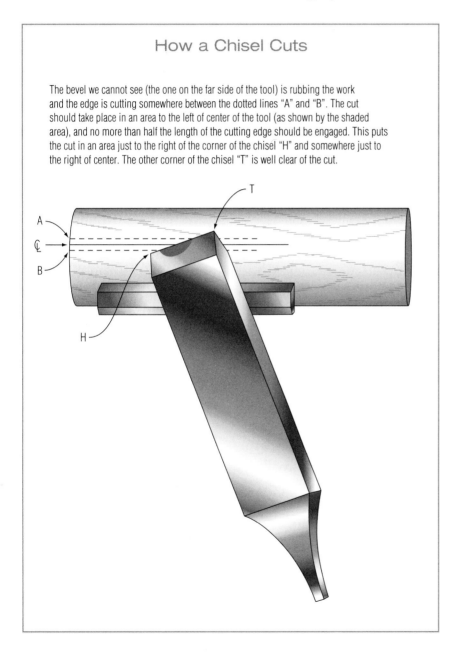

leave nasty craters in the work. Although I like to think that there are no mistakes, only new design opportunities, chisels catch with such gusto that the work is often ruined.

With that said, it is useful to purposely catch the chisel to learn the dynamics of the process. (This exercise can be done just as well with a skew chisel as with a traditional chisel.) Set the lathe to a very low speed, making sure the work is securely held between centers. If using a skew, make sure your left hand is on your side of the tool rest because skews can pinch the fleshy part of your hand against the rest in a catch. (I typically hold the tool loosely with my left hand in back of the rest.) With your right hand, raise the handle slowly upward to cause a catch—along with a new design opportunity.

SKEW CHISELS

Historically called long-corner chisels, skew chisels have two advantages over traditional chisels that make them easier to control. First, the handle may be brought at nearly right angles to the work, which allows you to stand directly behind the shank of the tool. Second, a skew also does not have to be tipped to quite as high an angle from where its edge contacts the rest as a traditional chisel does.

Beginners should start with a fairly wide skew that is 1 in. to $1\frac{1}{2}$ in. One (among many) of the problems with sets is that the skew is generally in the $\frac{1}{2}$-in. to $\frac{3}{4}$-in. range. Those skews are far too narrow for easy control, even in skilled hands. I have three skews: a $1\frac{1}{4}$ in., a 1 in., and a $\frac{1}{2}$ in. I use the 1 in. 90 percent of the time and only resort to $1\frac{1}{4}$ in. for large architectural work. I use the $\frac{1}{2}$-in. one, which does not even have a handle, in very tight quarters such as when cleaning up a shoulder next to a bead.

A skew is one of the few turning tools that is generally delivered with the correct bevel angles and grind (see the illustration at left on the facing page). However, the rectangular section the chisel is made from is usually achieved by Blanchard grinding, which leaves the corners of the rectangle sharp. Sharp corners do not slide along the tool rest, making the tool unpleasant to use as well as uncomfortable to hold. The illustration at right on the facing page shows what I call a "tuned" skew, where the corners of the rectangle have been given a healthy radius in the grinder then polished smooth.

Although you seldom have to grind a skew to start, you will have to regrind it if the tool has a hollow grind or if it has had dealings with a chuck. It is a simple matter to grind a flat bevel of the correct angle on any bench grinder, but the method will bring a cry from the grinder-safety people. That's because grinding a flat bevel requires grinding on the side of the wheel even though all modern grinding manuals say to grind only on the periphery of the wheel.

Start with a Big Skew

To make learning easier, start with a 1-in. (or even wider) skew chisel.

Skew Chisels

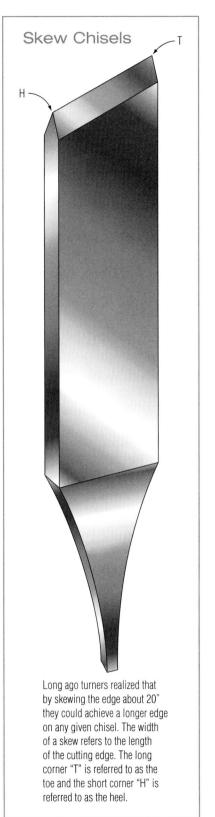

T

H

Long ago turners realized that by skewing the edge about 20° they could achieve a longer edge on any given chisel. The width of a skew refers to the length of the cutting edge. The long corner "T" is referred to as the toe and the short corner "H" is referred to as the heel.

A Tuned Skew

Radius edges

The safety people are worried that an unskilled turner will put excessive side pressure on a thin wheel, causing it to break. They are also worried that the same person might excessively dress the side of the wheel, possibly dressing a groove that could start a general fault in the wheel—a break on the dotted line so to speak. But I have never known an experienced toolmaker who did not grind on the side of a wheel once in a while. In addition, hardware stores sell twist-drill sharpening jigs that only work by using the side of a wheel.

The important thing is to bring some common sense to the situation. An occasional grinding on the side of a wheel is okay if you put only light side pressure on a ½-in. or wider wheel (the wider the better). Never excessively dress the side of a wheel. I typically lightly dress the sides of a wheel with a diamond dresser to true it up when I first mount it, then only dress once or twice more with a diamond during the entire life of the wheel. Always keep the grinding shields properly adjusted, and wear safety glasses or, even better, a face shield with safety glasses.

To grind a skew, set the rest so that it is level, and use this as a place to rest the shank of the tool for support. When grinding on the side of the wheel, there is a tendency for the top half of the tool to be ground less than the bottom, so you'll need to compensate for this by putting additional pressure on the top half. I typically apply pressure with my thumb against the top half. As you grind, alternate from one bevel to the other until an edge is formed and you have contiguous flat. Start with a

Grinding a skew on the side of a wheel is the only way to obtain a flat bevel. Grinder manufacturers don't recommend this, but it is safe if you use moderate pressure against a wheel that is ½ in. or wider.

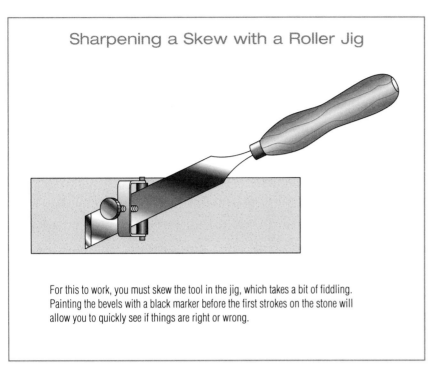

Sharpening a Skew with a Roller Jig

For this to work, you must skew the tool in the jig, which takes a bit of fiddling. Painting the bevels with a black marker before the first strokes on the stone will allow you to quickly see if things are right or wrong.

42° angle, then as your skill increases, lengthen both bevels to as long as 26° inclusive. You will have to approximate the correct angle, but you can cut out a 42° angle on cardboard for comparison.

The cutting edge also needs to be honed on whetstones, which you do in the same way as you would sharpen a plane iron. Simply stone both bevels on progressively finer stones until a polish is achieved. It helps to get your hands very close to the edge so that you can feel that the bevel is flat on the stone. A roller-type jig may help, but you will have to align the roller to the skewing angle of the chisel as shown in the illustration above.

Many turners today like to grind their skews to a curved edge. I do not like this grind for several reasons. First, it is more difficult to achieve the curved grind with a flat bevel, which is still necessary if the tool is going to perform well. Second, it is much more difficult to achieve a keen edge with whetstones on the curved edge. Third, the curved edge does not cut up to a shoulder well. Finally, the curved grind tends to exacerbate harmonic chatter on thin spindles.

How much the tool is turned toward the cutting direction is largely a matter of work diameter. You can achieve a better cut by keeping the handle as square to the work as possible, with the understanding that it can almost never be perfectly square (see the illustration on p. 130). You have to sufficiently skew the edge to the centerline to keep the toe clear of the cut. As the work diameter increases, you must increase the skewing angle by turning the tool further left and moving the handle right. At still-larger diameters, you have to go to a wider skew because the toe will no longer clear the cut.

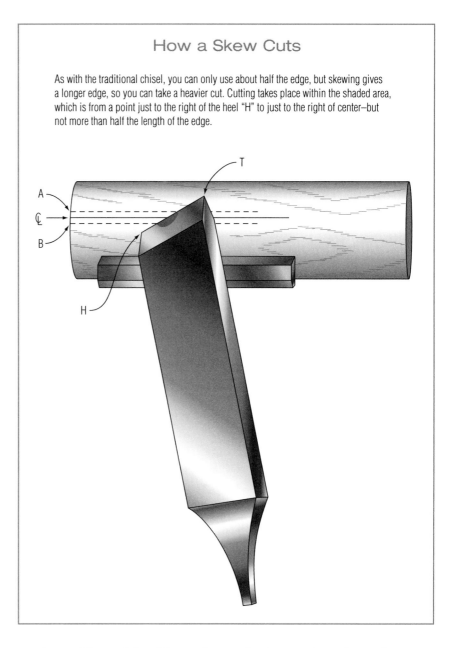

How a Skew Cuts

As with the traditional chisel, you can only use about half the edge, but skewing gives a longer edge, so you can take a heavier cut. Cutting takes place within the shaded area, which is from a point just to the right of the heel "H" to just to the right of center–but not more than half the length of the edge.

Long, thin work is subject to harmonic chatter where the work vibrates between centers, causing a spiral ripple in the finish. The more the edge is skewed to the work, the more harmonic chatter is exacerbated. Therefore, you should keep the handle of the skew as square to the work as possible.

A flat bevel contacts the centerline from the cutting edge to the heel of the bevel. If the edge is hollow-ground, there is no support for the cutting edge between where the heel of the bevel contacts the centerline and where the edge is cutting (which is also on the centerline). Therefore, a flat bevel makes the tool much more stable.

OVAL SKEWS

A rectangular skew chisel is difficult to use because the tool is unbalanced. The center of gravity is not under the downward movements of force because only one edge of the tool can contact the rest. An oval skew changes all of this. It creates a skew with a center of gravity that is nearly under the center of force—a center of gravity that is free to change with the rolling action of the tool.

Unfortunately, most oval skews are delivered with too long a bevel (26°) for most beginners. The problem can be fixed, though, by shortening the bevels to about 42°.

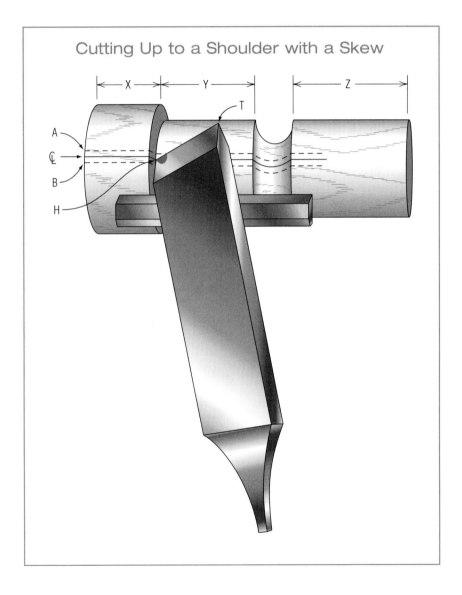

Cutting Up to a Shoulder with a Skew

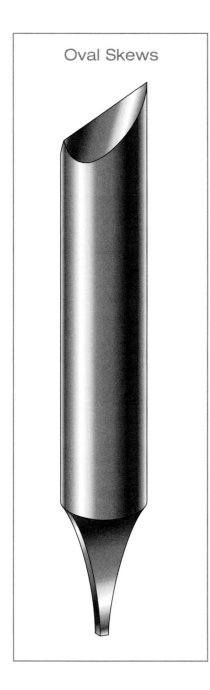

Oval Skews

Heel Cuts

TO OVERCOME HARMONIC CHATTER, you can use a heel cut. I generally wrap my hands around the work and hold the tool down on the rest with my thumb. I never grip the work so tightly that my hands get the least warm, although my flesh provides a dampening action that greatly reduces harmonic chatter. I think this hold also increases the pressure of the bevel against the work so that the tool effectively acts as its own steady rest. This is also why it is best to use a wide skew. The wider edge puts the toe further out of harm's way. At some point, only a steady rest will solve harmonic problems (and sometimes not entirely), but the combination of the heel cut and hands cradling the work will often carry the day.

You also need to use a heel cut if you must roll beads with a skew. I think this job is much more safely and effectively accomplished with the spindle gouge, but many seem to feel that rolling beads with a skew is some sort of rite of passage. I encourage you to try it on some scrap. You will find that the trick is using the heel cut and staying exactly on the bevel. Some turners roll beads with the toe, believing this is easier. I do not agree; you are just reversing the heel and toe, and since it is a heel cut that is necessary to roll a bead, the same dynamics apply.

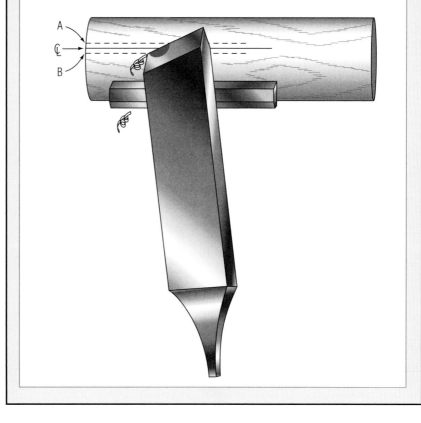

Wrapping you hands around the work and using a heel cut are good ways to overcome harmonic chatter. Properly done there should be a small shaving issuing from the heel, and the tool should be as square to the work as possible.

Cutoff Tools

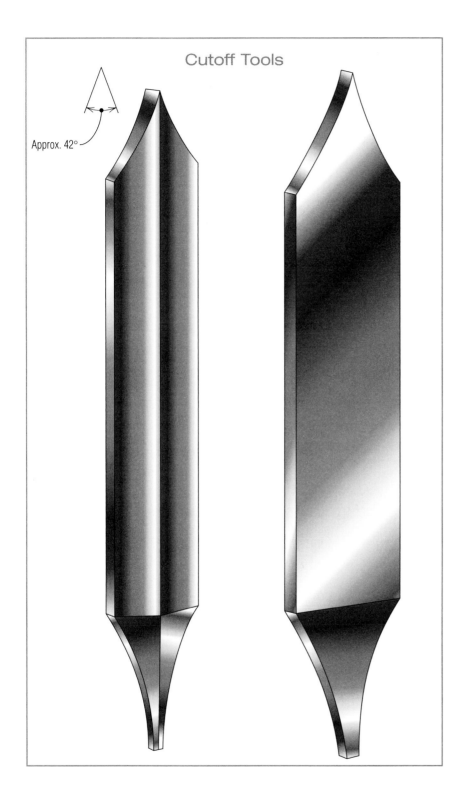

Approx. 42°

A Cutoff Tool in Action

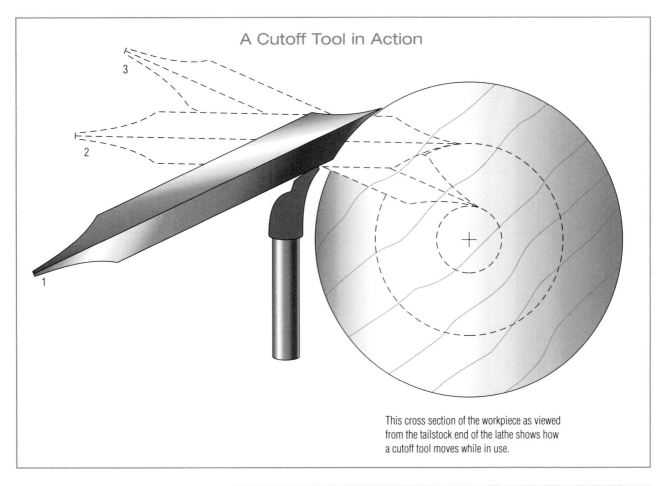

This cross section of the workpiece as viewed from the tailstock end of the lathe shows how a cutoff tool moves while in use.

A cutoff tool is easy to grind by eye. Simply touch both bevels to the grinder to achieve a 42° or less point, inclusive. Keep the point centered on the blank, especially on diamond tools.

CUTOFF TOOLS

The cutoff tool, sometimes called a parting tool, is also in the chisel family (see the illustration on p. 133). A diamond-shaped cutoff tool is the best variation of the tool, although it also comes in a cheaper rectangular variety. The diamond shape has several advantages. It presents less surface area to rub (thus creating less friction in a deep cutoff); it will still

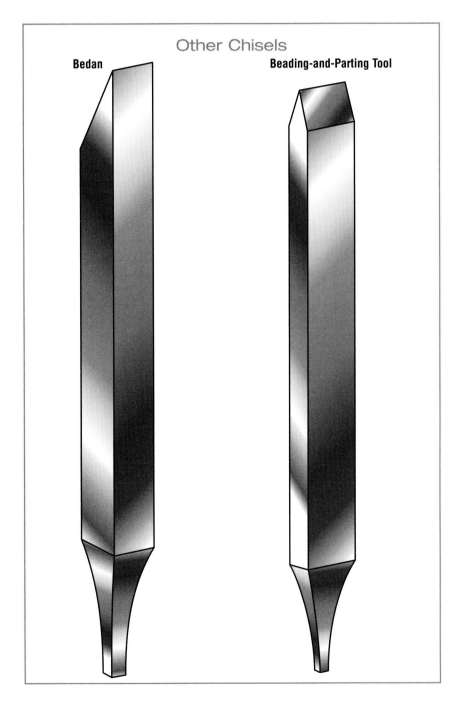

Other Chisels

Bedan

Beading-and-Parting Tool

cut if the tool is not perfectly vertical on the tool rest; and it cuts a narrower kerf in faceplate-oriented cutoffs. The chief advantage of the rectangular version is its low cost. Both types are generally sold in widths ranging from $\frac{1}{16}$ in. to $\frac{1}{4}$ in. wide.

Because of the way a cutoff tool is presented, you can hollow-ground it; it is best ground to a long double bevel of 42° or less, inclusive (see the photo on p. 134). Although most turners use the tool directly from the grinder, it works better in spindle work if you remove the burr by honing it on a fine stone.

To use a cutoff tool, place it vertically on the tool rest and present it at a high angle with the bevel rubbing and the edge just cutting. Rock it down until the cutting edge ends up at the exact center of the work and a parting is achieved. As you can see in the illustration on p. 134, the tool has to slide forward on the rest as the cutoff progresses to keep the bevel rubbing. In a deep cutoff, it is best to take overlapping cuts to keep the kerf wider than the tool. Presenting the tool this way in facework may result in a catch, so for faceplate cutoffs, present the tool at or slightly above the centerline and push it forward to the center.

CONE SEPARATION TOOLS

The cone separation tool is nothing more than a giant cutoff tool. It is used for cutting away the interior of a bowl to save time and wood. By coning away the center of a bowl, more bowls can be turned from the same blank. I often mount a thick blank and cone three nesting bowls from it.

You use this tool the same way as a cutoff tool in facework, but you will have to make overlapping cuts to keep the kerf considerably wider than the shank of the tool. Keep the belt slack so that if there is a jam due to chip buildup, the lathe will slip rather than break your arm. A cone separation tool should never be used with a gear-driven lathe.

OTHER TYPES OF CHISELS

The bedan and beading-and-parting tool also fit in the chisel family (see the illustration on p. 135). A bedan is much like a $\frac{3}{8}$-in.-wide bench chisel. It is essentially a superwide cutoff tool (though it is single beveled) and is used with exactly the same technique. The single bevel is ground to a long bevel, about 25° to 30°, inclusive. Like the parting tool, it can be hollow-ground but must be honed to a razor-sharp edge like the skew. It is handy for sizing tenons.

The beading-and-parting tool is basically a $\frac{3}{8}$-in.-wide traditional woodturner's chisel. It can be used both for sizing tenons and for rolling beads, but for the latter it must have a flat bevel. Like a skew, it must be used with a heel cut when rolling beads, but it may be a bit more controllable than a skew for this task.

Scrapers

The term scraper refers to a whole class of tools that are purposely sharpened to a burr and used at a downhill slant. The word scrape is misleading because in reality a scraper is taking a highly positive shear cut. A turner's scraper works exactly as a common cabinet scraper. The burr is what does the work because it is actually a micro cutting edge (see the illustration on p. 138). The short length of the burr effectively limits the depth of cut per revolution of the work, making it a safe, predictable tool.

There are times when it is impossible to use a gouge, so a scraper is called for. Scrapers are the workaday implements that get the job done—and often carry the day. A gouge may be the best way to cut wood because it leaves the best finish, but it requires a fair amount of skill and cannot reach blind areas. A scraper cuts wood handily in all situations and requires only a modicum of skill. You can also grind scrapers to complicated shapes, making it easy to duplicate details.

A scraper is quite different from other turning tools, and at first it can be a little unnerving to use. Up until now, you have been taught to shear-cut, which requires keeping the bevel of the tool rubbing on the work surface. Suddenly, you must now point the tool downhill and drag the burred edge for it to cut properly. In fact, pointing it uphill can cause a nasty catch.

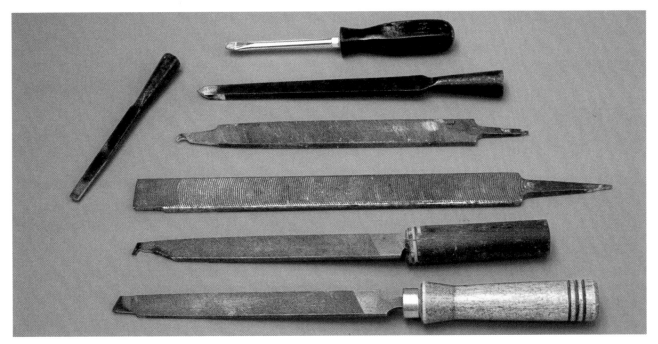

Scrapers are sharpened to a burr, which is dragged across the work at a downward slope. A scraper can be made from almost any piece of steel, a screw drive, a cement nail, an Allen wrench, or an old piece of spring steel. Here is a collection of scrapers I have either bought or improvised over the years.

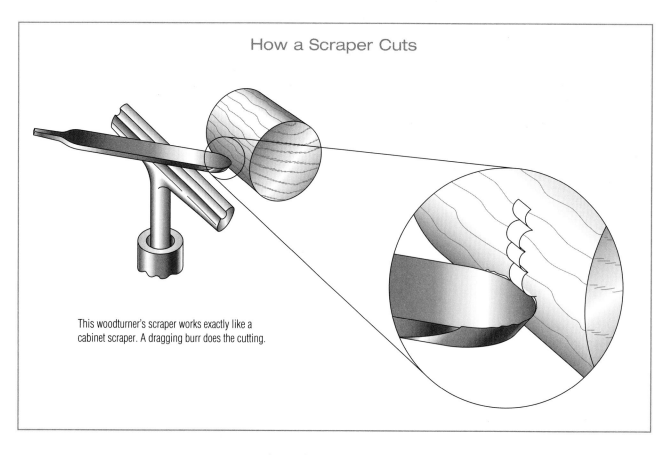

How a Scraper Cuts

This woodturner's scraper works exactly like a cabinet scraper. A dragging burr does the cutting.

The trick of using a scraper effectively is to point it slightly downhill and touch it lightly to the work. Inside a bowl it is necessary to raise the rest a bit for the tool to point downhill but to cut on the centerline. You will have to play around with how far downhill you slant your scraper depending on how you created the burr. Burnished burrs need more slant than ground burrs, and no two people burnish exactly the same way. The trick is to find the right angle for your sharpening methods.

Simply pointing the tool slightly downhill is not always enough, though, especially when using a dome scraper on the inside of a bowl. If you start a scraping cut at the inside center, your concentration is naturally on the tip of the tool. As you approach the sidewall of the bowl, the side of the scraper starts to cut. If you do not pay attention, you may find the side of the tool cutting uphill instead of downhill and a catch may occur. The trick is either to swing the handle to the right, roll the tool on the rest, or both.

You should hold a scraper loosely in your fingers and place it ever so lightly against the work. If a scraper is pushed, it goes from a positive-angle cut by the burr to a negative-angle plow cut, with tearout aplenty. For heavy faceplate work, the heavier the scraper the better. For bowl work, I have a dome scraper made out of an old jackhammer chisel. It weighs about 5 lb. and never jumps around on the rest.

A scraper is one of the easiest tools to grind.

Grind to shape using your pattern as a guide. Everything should be undercut at least 5° but no more than 15°.

Making a Form Scraper

You can make a form scraper by drawing the shape you want on a piece of paper, gluing the resulting pattern to the scraper, and grinding to the pattern.

There are two ways to sharpen a scraper: grinding and burnishing. Grinding a scraper is simplicity itself. Set the grinding rest so that the bevel will be ground to about a 75° inclusive angle (most turners refer to this as 15° of clearance in the edge). Place the tool flat on the rest, and push it into the wheel. Keeping firm pressure on the tool, swing it to achieve the desired shape (see the bottom photo above). You do not need

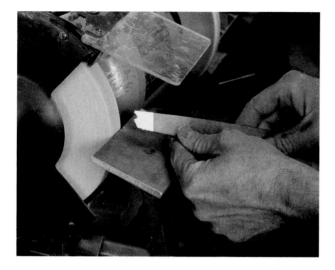

When the scraper is ground, it should look like this. Note the undercut is also about 5° to the sides in the area of the bead.

to grind the tool upside down to achieve the burr; it forms just as well by grinding right side up and you can see what is happening. A burr is the natural outcome any time a tool is ground.

Even though a ground burr works quite well, burnishing creates an even better burr. A burnish is no more than a round or oval bar of hard, polished steel. It is like a file without teeth. When burnishing a commercially available scraper, you must use a carbide burnisher because a standard cabinetmaker's burnisher will only work if a tool is soft enough—around 55 HRC. HSS turning tools (scrapers included) are in the range of 58 HRC to 62 HRC.

It is possible, though, to make a scraper from a softer piece of metal and burnish it successfully with a cabinetmaker's burnisher. You can also draw the temper back on an old file to make it soft enough to burnish. To do this, grind the file to the desired shape and buff the area adjacent to the cutting edge to a good polish. Carefully and evenly heat the file with a propane torch until the polished area turns a deep blue color. Keep the torch moving all the time, and do not apply too much heat at the cutting edge. You should apply more heat behind the edge so that the heat flows out to the edge. When the tip area is bright blue, quench it in water. You have now drawn the temper back to about 55 HRC and can burnish with a standard cabinetmaker's burnisher.

The burnishing process changes the crystalline structure of the steel at the cutting edge, increasing the hardness in this area. This is called work-hardening. It is not possible to burnish without first removing this work-hardened area by filing or grinding it away. Once the cutting edge has been filed or ground, use an oil stone to bring the bevel and the back (top surface) of the tool to a good finish. It need not be a polish, just a good

Burnishing a Scraper

Burnishing a turning scraper is much the same as burnishing a cabinet scraper. It is a three-step process: grinding away the old, work-hardened edge; bringing the ground edge to a hard, polished corner with oil stones; and burnishing a burr with a burnishing tool.

1 Grind to remove the work-hardened metal at the edge.

2 Use an oil stone to bring the bevel and back to a good finish.

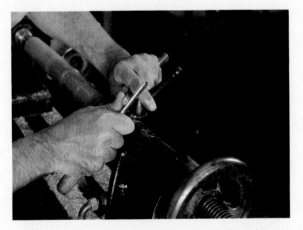

3 Use a cabinetmaker's burnisher to roll the edge. Considerable force is necessary, and a bit of wax helps in rolling the burr because it makes the burnish slide more easily. You may find clamping the tool in a vise helpful.

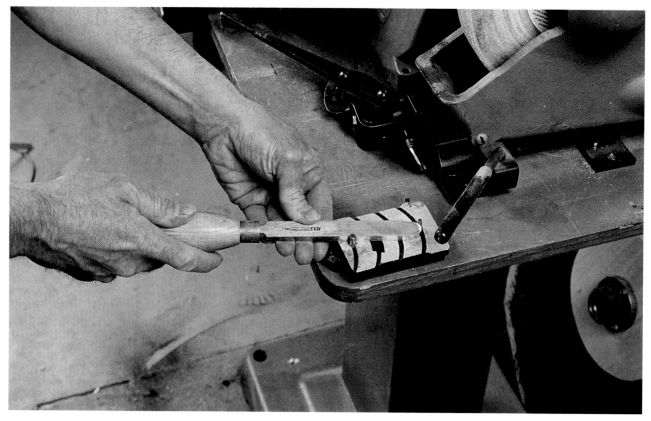

Veritas makes a burnishing fixture that will roll a burr even on HSS scrapers.

Using a Burnished Scraper

You may have to tip a burnished scraper further downhill to get it to cut than a ground scraper.

finish. Next, rub the burnish along the bevel edge with considerable force. By slanting the burnish toward the back of the tool, you roll a burr. To get sufficient leverage, you may find it necessary to clamp the tool in a bench vise and place some body weight on the burnish. Waxing or oiling the burnish also helps because it reduces friction.

Although burnishing works well and produces a burr superior to grinding, it is not worth the trouble on small scrapers, especially if a scraper has a complicated shape. When doing heavy faceplate work with a large scraper, a burnished burr offers considerable advantages because it takes heavier shavings and holds it edge slightly longer.

Veritas makes a burnishing fixture that will roll a burr even on HSS scrapers (see the photo above). It employs a carbide cone fixed in an aluminum base, which screws to a work surface. A fulcrum pin, which can be located in two positions, allows you to lever the cutting edge of any tool against the carbide cone to roll the burr. The fixture works well and is inexpensive.

Hook and Ring Tools

Hook tools and their easier-to-manufacture modern equivalents, ring tools, are left over from the time when lathes were human powered. The easiest way to visualize a hook tool is to think of bending the leading inch of a roughing-out gouge up at a right angle (see the illustration below). This configuration allows you to present the edge of the tool at the bottom of a bowl. The tool is most prevalent in Scandinavia, where its use has never entirely died out.

If properly sharpened, hook tools are efficient, but they are designed for very low speeds such as those you would encounter in spring-pole lathes. I cannot emphasize enough that speeds of 150 rpm to 250 rpm are a must when using this tool for faceplate work. Hooks are dangerous at high turning speeds.

To use the tool, place it level (or even pointed slightly downhill) on the rest. Roll it left about 45° so that the face of the cutting edge is

Hook and Ring Tools

Scandinavian turners use a fulcrum pin to aid in levering a tool in an arc. The tool is rolled 45° left during use.

Rest

Fulcrum pin

Typical forged hook tool, which is still used in Scandinavia

Sorby's ring tool is turned, and shank is welded to the ring.

The Termite, Oneway's ring tool, is investment cast and mechanically attached to the shank.

You can use the Sorby chatter tool to do decorative chatter on end grain, such as on the box lid shown here.

pointed to about 10 o'clock, and swing it in an arc to create bowls. In Scandinavia, turners put a fulcrum pin in the middle of their tool rests to lever the shank of the hook. This makes the tool both more efficient and easier to swing in a pleasing arc. For faceplate work on a modern lathe, I do not find hooks as efficient as a good HSS bowl gouge.

Hooks work in hollow spindle work, too, and will tolerate higher speed here. They are great for turning the insides of goblets, eggcups, and scoops. However, I do not find them any more efficient than a spindle gouge ground to a long fingernail and turned 45° to the left. With either a spindle gouge or a hook, you present the tool at the center, lever it sidewise, and drag it up the wall of the goblet or cup.

Ring tools are essentially the same as hook tools, but they lend themselves better to modern manufacturing methods. The ring may be turned on a screw machine and the handle spot-welded or mechanically fastened. Smaller rings are often investment cast. The one drawback to small ring tools over true hooks is that chips do not always clear through the ring well, thus the tool stops cutting due to chip backup.

Hooks and ring tools are best sharpened with a small grinding wheel mounted in a Dremel tool. Grind only the inside surfaces of the ring or hook.

Chatter Tools

A chatter tool is nothing more than a small, round-nose (or sometimes V-shape) scraper made from thin stock that vibrates when the tool is brought into play. The vibration creates interesting decorative patterns that are cut into end grain. The tool is often used to put decorations on box lids and to add fun embellishment on knobs. However, the technique only works on end grain of fairly substantial wood.

Making a Chatter Tool

You can make a quick and dirty chatter tool by clamping a length of industrial-power hacksaw blade (or any spring steel of comparable thickness) in a pair of vise grips used as a handle. Or you can make a wooden handle if you want a nicer look.

The thin stock is mechanically clamped in a substantial handle. The frequency at which the tool resonates is controlled by how far it is extended out of the handle and by the speed of your lathe. Short extensions and greater speeds result in high frequency and vice versa. To get the right pattern, you need to fiddle with the extension of the tool from the handle and with the lathe speed. You can also change the pattern by presenting the tool in different locations—above center, on center, and below center. Presenting the tool on center gives straight chatter marks, while positioning it above or below causes the pattern to swirl in opposite directions. The tool is readily available in woodworking-supply catalogs, but it's easy to make a shop-built version.

Chasers

The classic way to cut screw threads in the lathe is by chasing, which requires a lathe that can be taken to very low speed and a set of chasers. Chasers are sold in sets: one for internal threads and one for external. Years ago, they were offered in just about any thread pitch imaginable, but today they are only offered in 16, 18, and 20 pitch. For most wood situations, 16 or 18 is about right. Chasers are available from Craft Supplies (see Resources on p. 184).

In the past, threads were just as likely to be chased in bone, ivory, or horn because turners used these materials often. Chasing requires wood of exceptional properties, such as boxwood, dogwood, persimmon, pear, or, in a pinch, maple. Many tropical species also work well for chasing. All of these woods are exceptionally dense and tight-grained, allowing threading without crumbling along the grain.

Shown here is a set of antique thread chasers, but you may purchase new chasers from Craft Supplies.

The trick to chasing is to start with only the face of the tool against the work and the cutting edge clear of the cut. Then gradually tip the tool down until the edge engages and a thread is cut.

The business end of a chaser looks much like a thick sawblade except the teeth are angled at the pitch angle of the thread to be chased. The trick to using a chaser is to set the lathe to a *very* low speed (5 rpm to 10 rpm) and tip the scraper up so that the angled face (edge of the teeth) engages the wood but the actual cutting edge is clear of the cut. Because the teeth are at the pitch angle of the thread, the tool will move sideways as the work turns. You need to apply a firm inward pressure (or outward pressure for internal threads) to chase a deep line in the area to be threaded. Additionally, you must apply some sideways force to make the chaser cut at the correct pitch.

Next, return the chaser to the beginning of the thread, and pick up the lines that you have previously incised. The instant the thread is picked up, tip the tool down to bring the edge into play in a scrape cut (see the photo above). Again, some sideways pressure is necessary to maintain pitch. Return the chaser to the start and repeat the process until a perfect thread is formed. Internal threading is more difficult because you cannot easily see what is happening.

If you are threading to a shoulder (as in boxes), redrawing the chaser at the precise moment is also required. In other words, very low speed is a must. For those lacking a variable-speed lathe, an old trick for this kind of work is to mount the motor on a swing arm controlled by a foot pedal. Pushing down on the pedal lifts the motor and slackens the belt. Releasing the pedal drops the motor and tightens the belt, giving normal power. This allows fine nuances of power and speed. Often a spring or counterweight provides proper belt tension during normal use, but this scheme only works with V-belts.

Threading Options

If you have a metal-cutting lathe, you can mill threads on it. Simply set up the gearing for the pitch you wish to cut, then mount a laminate router in the tool post. Run the lathe by hand by manually advancing the drive belt. Another way to mill threads is to use a wood-lathe attachment such as the Nova ornamental (see p. 108).

Maintenance, Repair, and Modification

W hen you buy a new car, you spend the first few thousand miles "breaking it in" and the rest of its life "wearing it out." So it is with a lathe. Maintenance is required on a regular basis, and sooner or later repair is necessary. Maintenance and repair are tasks that most of us tend to neglect for one reason or another. My sense is that most people aren't quite sure what to do. In this chapter, I'll explain what must be done to keep your lathe running in tip-top condition and suggest some things that may make it run even better.

This chapter is also intended as an aid to buying a used lathe. A machine with a few years under its V-, poly-V-, or flat belt often represents an exceptional value and may possess features you would have to pay a lot for in a new machine. My father and I have purchased many classic lathes (wood and metal) at bargain prices, and all have more than lived up to our expectations. As my father aptly sums it up, "In former times, honest construction was the rule, and manufacturers weren't afraid to pour a little metal in the mold." Like the Rolls Royce salesman, I like to think of classic machines not as used but as previously owned. A little love and maintenance will restore such machines to their original conditions.

Routine Maintenance

Fortunately, a lathe doesn't require a great deal of maintenance and even thrives in an environment of downright neglect. There are some habits you can form and some things you can do that will greatly add to the life

LATHE MAINTENANCE SCHEDULE

Frequency	Task	Reason
Every time you use a Morse-taper accessory	Wipe dust out of the taper socket with your finger and wipe the taper accessory.	The biggest cause of spindle damage (headstock and tailstock) is damaged tapers or taper seats due to dirt.
Every turning session	Sweep or vacuum chips from the machine, then wax all unpainted metal parts such as the bed, spindles, and tool rest. Oil plane bearings. If your machine has oil holes or cups, you should apply a few drops of a high-viscosity (30 or higher) machine oil. Some older motors also have oil cups, which should be lubricated.	Wood is hygroscopic and even dry wood can promote rusting in the right conditions. If you turn green wood, this action is an absolute must. Plane bearings will run forever if lubricated. They require a film of oil; if they don't have it, they will quickly fail.
Monthly	Grease any zerk fittings. Some older machines may have grease fittings for the headstock bearings and possibly the motor. They should be given one shot of grease. Do not overgrease. This should be a habit.	Grease is required on a regular basis to keep such bearings healthy.
Annually	Clean all belt pulleys.	Dirt and rubber buildup on pulleys causes vibration.
Every one to five years	Check the belt for wear and the bearings for endplay and lubrication. On most lathes that are used a reasonable amount, this check should be done more frequently. Since the spindle has to be removed on most lathes to replace the belt, you might as well replace the bearings. On variable-width sheave machines, belt replacement will be required every year or two, so replacing the bearings may not make sense in this case.	A worn or loose belt causes vibration and poor power transmission. Dry bearings will soon fail (if they have not already).
Every decade regardless of use	Replace the belt and bearings.	Time alone will take its toll. Grease in sealed bearings will dry out, and rubber in belts gets hard and cracks.

of your machine and to your enjoyment of using it. The first habit is to unplug the machine when you perform most maintenance. Other habits follow different schedules (see the chart above). Routine maintenance will keep your machine running smoothly for years.

Replacing Bearings

In the unlikely event that you have an old lathe with plane bearings, you can keep the lathe running smoothly by oiling the bearings on a daily basis. Most lathes today, even those found on the used market, are equipped with ball bearings that are lubricated and "sealed for life." These bearings don't require any regular maintenance, but they do need to be replaced every few years.

The sides of ball bearings are generally sealed with plastic, which retains the grease packed into the bearing during assembly. Age and use take their toll on any grease, even in a sealed-for-life bearing. Eventually, the grease fails and the bearing fails shortly thereafter. I've always joked that a sealed-for-life bearing is just that: It's sealed for its life, which is however long it takes for the grease to fail. Fortunately, this is typically a good, long time.

If you use your lathe on a regular basis, you probably won't notice the gradual loss of bearing performance. If your bearings are more than five years old, however, chances are they're anemic, if not spent, and it's time to think about replacing them. A good test for worn bearings is to remove tension from the belt, which leaves the headstock spindle free to turn without resistance. Spin the spindle by placing your hand on the pulley. If the spindle spins freely and the bearings have a "dry" sound and feel, the grease is dry. (If the grease is still good, the spindle will have a slightly dead feel and not want to spin freely.) The first order of business is to remove the offending bearings.

I can't offer a definite prescription for removing bearings since no two headstock designs are the same. However, understanding how a typical bearing assembly goes together should help you figure out any headstock. The surfaces of the bearings and the bearing seats (the areas on the spindle where the bearings ride and the pockets in the headstock that hold them) are machined to strict tolerances.

There are two types of fit for the bearing seats: a sliding fit and a press fit. In a sliding fit, the two mating surfaces can slide over each other, but there is no radial play. In a press fit, a slightly larger diameter is pressed into a slightly smaller mating diameter. The difference is typically on the order of 0.0005 in. Such assemblies require an arbor press to put them together (see the photo above).

Because the headstock spindle expands as it heats up during use, at least one of the bearing seats must be a slide fit. A common configuration is shown in the illustration on p. 150. The bearings are a press fit into the headstock casting, and the front bearing is a press fit against the shoulder on the spindle. (The other side of this shoulder is the shoulder for the nose thread.) The back bearing is a slide fit with the spindle.

Most lathes have additional fittings to hold and cover the bearings. Often, metal rings screw into place with three or more screws around the

An arbor press is generally necessary to press bearings on and off of shafts, but you can improvise a European-style workbench into an arbor press.

Buying Bearings
You can typically get bearings that are less expensive from a bearing supplier than from the manufacturer of your lathe.

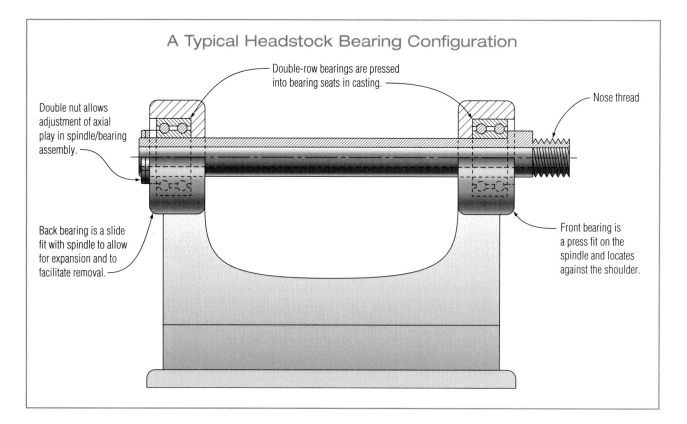

A Typical Headstock Bearing Configuration

Double-row bearings are pressed into bearing seats in casting.

Nose thread

Double nut allows adjustment of axial play in spindle/bearing assembly.

Back bearing is a slide fit with spindle to allow for expansion and to facilitate removal.

Front bearing is a press fit on the spindle and locates against the shoulder.

spindle, and these may contain seals that further protect the bearing. A common design is to have a fine thread on the back of the spindle (the end opposite the nose) on which there are two nuts. The first nut runs up against the inner race of the bearing and is adjusted until there is no play in the assembly. The second nut is then locked against the first.

Sometimes a wavy washer is interposed between the nuts and the bearing as well, its purpose being to remove play from the assembly. This washer should be replaced with the bearings because it invariably takes a set. Snap rings are used extensively today, and there are typically an array of spacers and washers involved. As you disassemble the headstock, make a careful sketch of the order in which you take off all of these parts so that you can reassemble everything correctly.

Once you've taken the headstock apart, there are a variety of ways to remove the bearings from the spindle. One method is to use a bearing puller (see the photo on the facing page). A tool of this type would be used for removing the back bearing, and possibly the front, from the typical headstock shown in the illustration above. To remove a press-fit bearing from the spindle, you'll normally need an arbor press. Often the entire headstock must be placed in a press.

If you have a European-style workbench, it's not difficult to improvise an arbor press (see the photo essay on pp. 152–153). Using the bench dogs in combination with arbors and support blocks, both turned and fabricated from durable wood, will provide the necessary support and force you need to remove the bearings from the spindle.

Support blocks can be made in one of two ways. One is to nail and glue up a right-angle plate from scrap wood. I used such a plate in the photo essay of replacing the bearings in a Delta headstock on pp. 152–153. The second way is to mount a square block in a four-jaw chuck and drill a hole through it to a diameter slightly larger than the spindle (1⅛ in. for the spindle assembly in the photos). Then scrape a pocket in the support block to accept the bearing.

To make an arbor, turn a hickory or oak billet to a tenon with a shoulder. The tenon diameter should be equal to the inside diameter of the shaft. Clamp the support block to the workbench, insert the tenon into the spindle, then use the tail vise to force the spindle out of the headstock or bearing.

Although it's tempting to pound the assembly apart using soft-faced mallets and blocks of wood, I strongly urge you not to do this because this practice can ruin the bearings by putting flat spots on the balls. Although it makes no difference in the disassembly, it does in the assembly. Since one is merely the reverse of the other, it's not a good habit to get into—in my opinion, hammers have no place around bearings. Once the bearings are out, test them by spinning them with your hand. If the grease is dry, the bearing will spin and even coast for a while; if it's really bad, you'll feel flat spots in the bearing.

Replacement bearings are easy to obtain. Each bearing will have a shield number on one or both sides, which should be all the information a bearing supplier will need to get you a replacement. For instance, a 2802Z would be a double-row bearing that presses into a 1⅜-in. bearing seat and

Bearing pullers are used to remove the bearings from a headstock spindle. The puller at right is for removing small bearings from shaft assemblies, while the larger model at left can adjust to a variety of situations.

Replacing Bearings

This method uses a European-style workbench as an arbor press.

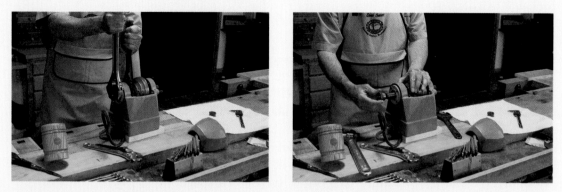

1 I start by removing the shoulder nuts from both ends of the spindle. Here I am removing the inboard nut. The outboard nut is left hand, so you need to turn in the opposite direction from normal.

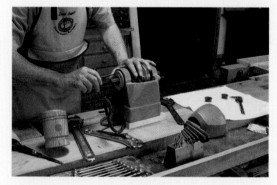

2 Next, I use a hex wrench to remove the flanges, which cover and protect the bearings.

3 Now I use an arbor and the tail vise to push the spindle and the outboard bearing out of the headstock. In this case, I was able to put the bench dog directly against the outboard end of the headstock and did not have to use a support block as I will for reassembly.

4 Using a wooden arbor (turned to the inside diameter of the inboard bearing) and a support block of scrap plywood, I remove the inboard bearing from its seat. I drilled a hole in the support block slightly bigger than the bearing's outside diameter.

5 While the headstock is apart, it is time to take care of rust. I use Klingspor's Sandflex blocks to remove corrosion. The blocks come in coarse, medium, and fine grits. I start with coarse and work to fine to obtain a close-to-new finish. Emery paper is also good for this purpose.

6 Now it's time to reverse the process to install the new bearings. I install the inboard bearing back on the spindle.

7 I push the outboard bearing back into the headstock.

8 To replace the arbor and inboard bearing, I first have to drill a hole in my support block for the indexing pin to go through. I also made an arbor that went over the spindle nose and pushed on the inboard bearing directly.

9 I push the arbor and inboard bearing into place.

10 Replace the shoulder nuts.

Shown here are outboard (left) and inboard (right) bearings with a wavy washer, which takes up play. The inboard bearing is wider because it is a double-row bearing that better takes the increased radial and axial loads at the inboard end of the spindle. By reading the shield numbers (located at the top on both bearings here), you can go to a bearing supplier and obtain replacements.

accepts a ⅝-in. shaft. Bearing suppliers are listed in the Yellow Pages (Bearing Distributors and Technico are two of the better-known companies). It never hurts to take the bearing along with you to the bearing store so you can check the replacement directly against the original. You'll be amazed at just how inexpensive a new set of bearings is—typically no more than $25.

Once you have the new bearings for your lathe, reassemble the spindle assembly and headstock in the reverse order that you took it apart. The correct sequence for reinstalling the bearings on a Delta headstock is shown in the photo essay on pp. 152–153.

In the rare event that you have a very old set of bearings for which replacements are no longer available, you may still be able to salvage the bearings. Such bearings are typically shielded with a metal disk on one side but not sealed. Once you have the bearings out of the headstock, soak them in kerosene or a similar solvent (in a well-ventilated area) to remove the old, dried grease and dirt. Never use compressed air on bearings since it normally ruins them. Using a soft brush and some elbow grease will remove the dirt just fine.

Next, heat up some grease in a metal can by using an electric hot plate. Be most careful of fire—I prefer to do this kind of work outside. Almost any good-quality automotive grease will work, but if you're a stickler for doing it right, you can get tubes of grease specially formulated for bearings at any bearing store. Drop the bearings in the liquid grease, and let them soak for a while. Once the grease cools, pull the bearings out, remove the excess, and you're back in business.

Although it's not a difficult job to replace bearings, not everyone has the proper tools for it. The best alternative to doing it yourself is to take the entire headstock to an automotive machine shop and have the work done for you. Automotive machine shops abound, and they're well equipped for any work involving bearing removal and replacement. On most lathes, the headstock is a separate piece that can be removed. If the headstock and bed are a one-piece casting, you'll have to take the entire machine to the shop. If you cannot find an automotive machine shop, check the Yellow Pages and the Internet for "Machinery Repair Companies."

Drive Pulleys, Belts, and Motors

Drive pulleys and belts can cause a good deal of trouble, even in new lathes. If a lathe has "as cast" die-cast pulleys (which are common on economy lathes), chances are that they are neither perfectly concentric nor round. Since V-belts grip on the flanks of the pulley groove, a dial indicator is of little or no use in checking accuracy. The best method is to turn the pulleys over by hand with a pointer held stationary in the groove. You can clamp a pointed object such as a scriber in a suitable place near the pulley. Any radial or side-to-side runout will be apparent through care-

---

Isolating Vibration

VIBRATION IS A PROBLEM that can cause great consternation, since turning is difficult if the machine and work are moving around. Vibration tends to be speed related—most lathes have a bit of vibration, usually at one or two specific speeds. This is one of the reasons I like variable speed. If the work itself is causing the vibration, tweaking the speed up or down a bit is an instant cure.

Pulleys and belts are the most common sources of vibration, so these are the first things to inspect. Check for worn belts and out-of-true pulleys. If these are in good shape, next check the dynamic balance of the rotating parts. The motor may even be out of balance; although this isn't a common problem, it does happen.

Vibration is often a problem on lathes that have sheet-metal stands. Pouring sand into the stand can work wonders, but you have to make sure that the sand doesn't get into the motor, pulleys, and other moving parts. (If you're pouring sand into the stand, make sure you leave some air space below the motor for cooling purposes.) Placing sand bags in the base of the machine will often do the trick. Stamped-metal legs can be reinforced by adding wood cross braces, and vibration can be dampened by draping sand bags over the cross members. Another alternative is to build a replacement plywood box stand for your lathe and fill the legs with sand (see the photo and illustration on p. 26).

Locating Vibration

A stethoscope is a useful tool for isolating difficult-to-find vibration.

Truing Die-Cast Pulleys in a Wood Lathe

If you have a lathe available while your lathe is apart, this is a good way to true a pulley.

2 Use a woodturning scraper ground to the correct shape to true the pulley grooves.

1 Mount the pulley on a stub arbor that has been turned from a square of hickory in a four-jaw scroll chuck. Further support the pulley with a live center. I also tighten the pulley grub screw to give a more positive drive.

3 The finished pulley.

ful observation. Concentricity tolerances for pulleys are quite loose—typically 0.005-in. to 0.006-in. minimum runout. If the runout is excessive (more than 0.010 in.) and your lathe is having vibration problems, the pulley is the likely culprit.

What you should do about pulleys that are out of true will depend largely on how much money you want to spend and how much trouble you're willing to go to. The best solution is to replace the defective pulleys with machined cast-iron models, which should last as long as your lathe. High-quality pulleys to fit most spindles are available at most bearing stores, but they'll be expensive ($30 to $60 each) and will have to be special-ordered. If your headstock spindle is an odd size, you may still have to have the arbor hole in the pulley bored out and a new keyway roached.

Another remedy is to have the pulleys machined by a local machine shop. I've also mounted die-cast pulleys in a wood lathe and machined the sides of the grooves with a scraper. I mount a suitable square of wood in a four-jaw scroll chuck such as the Nova or the Oneway (see p. 70). I then turn the end to a short stub arbor that's a press fit with the pulley. I push the pulley on the arbor and lock it there with the setscrew in the pulley, as shown in the photo essay on the facing page. I further support the pulley by bringing the tailstock up close and engaging a live center with a 60° point into the bore of the pulley. I now start the lathe and scrape the offending groove flanks true. It's really quite simple. However, since your lathe is apart there are some technical problems to overcome—you'll either have to do the work on a second lathe, or temporarily substitute a simple one-groove pulley for the one you're scraping.

Sometimes dirt and rubber from the belt will build up in the pulley grooves and cause the belt to make a "klunking" sound as it runs. This buildup can usually be removed with solvent, but sometimes it will require sanding or filing. Again, mounting the pulley on a stub arbor can help in this task. Finally, a pulley greatly out of balance can cause excessive vibration. Many automotive machine shops have dynamic balancing machines and can remedy the problem for you. For the headstock pulley, have both the spindle and the pulley balanced as a unit.

Belts are much like tires, ranging greatly in price and quality. The difference between discount-store belts and good belts is like the difference between bias-ply tires and radial tires. A cheap belt will be stiff and uneven in cross section and will often cause noise and vibration. You can obtain a high-quality replacement belt from a bearing store for less than $20; Gates Green Belts is a reliable brand. It's good shop practice to replace the belt whenever you replace the bearings and vice versa. Normally, you can expect to get two to five years of use out of a good belt, but less if your lathe has a variable-width pulley speed control.

The motor that powers your lathe may sometimes require attention. When faced with a motor that won't run, you have two options: repair it or replace it. Your nose will usually tell you if the motor is burned out—it will have a distinct electrical-fire smell. Unless the motor is underpowered to begin with, rewinding is typically a good option. A motor rewinder (look in the Yellow Pages or on the Internet) can rebuild the motor for $100 to $150. A rewinder can also help with other motor ills. Common problems with single-phase induction motors are burned-out starting winding, problems with the centrifugal starting switch, and a bad capacitor.

The best solution for a stuck Morse taper is to use a big hammer.

Removing Seized Morse Tapers and Faceplates

It's not uncommon for a Morse-taper accessory to become stuck in the headstock or tailstock spindle. This typically occurs when you slam a Morse taper hard into the socket when the spindle is hot after a bout of high-speed turning. The hot socket shrinks around the cold Morse-taper center. Running the lathe until it heats up again usually cures the problem, but if this doesn't work, more drastic measures are necessary.

The correct way to remove a Morse taper is to insert a knockout bar through the back of the spindle and drive it out with a snap of the wrist. If the Morse taper is stuck, however, repeated blows with a knockout bar will do no more than put flat spots in the bearings. The problem here is overcoming starting friction, and the best course of action is to get a heavy hammer and give the knockout bar one firm blow (which does less damage to the bearings than a series of light raps).

Once you have overcome starting friction, the rest of the force from your hammer blow goes into propelling the taper out of the spindle at high velocity. Have your other hand ready to catch the taper, or, if you're unsure of your catching abilities, hold a scrap board against it. For tapers seized in self-ejecting tailstocks, the spindle has to be removed so that a knockout bar can be placed against the taper.

A faceplate can also become frozen on the spindle thread. A common cause is not threading a heavily loaded plate all the way home when initially mounting it on the lathe. When the lathe is started, the faceplate is

Finding Morse-Taper Accessories

Morse-taper accessories such as drill chucks, live centers, and taper adapters (taper sleeves) can be found at machine-tool supply houses at very reasonable prices—often more reasonable than at your woodworking machine dealer.

screwed home with tremendous force. There are a number of remedies for this problem, the first being simply to get a bigger wrench. More leverage can be obtained by using a "cheater," which is a short length of pipe that is slipped over the handle of the wrench (see the photo below left). Where possible, rest the wrench for the spindle against the lathe bed or headstock casting to provide a rock-solid stop. If the cheater doesn't work, try hitting the wrench directly with a couple of blows from a lead or brass hammer.

If these methods fail, you'll have to resort to harsher remedies. Place a heavy brass bar against one flat of the faceplate nut and give it a sharp rap with a hammer (see the photo below right). The idea is to give the threaded portion of the faceplate a shocking blow at right angles to the axis of the thread, which will break up the molecular interaction between the two threads. If you go back to the wrenches, the faceplate will usually come right off.

In the unlikely event that no mechanical means will remove the seized faceplate, one final remedy is to use a propane torch to heat one flat of the threaded area (wear heavy leather gloves for this operation). It's important to heat only one small area of the plate, which will cause the circumference to expand much as if you form a circle with your thumb and index finger then push the two slightly apart at the tips. Avoid heating the spindle and bearings as much as possible. When the plate is hot, use a wrench to remove it.

A cheater will typically provide the extra leverage to remove a stubborn faceplate.

Delivering a solid blow to the edge of a faceplate with a hammer and brass drift often frees a frozen faceplate.

Tool Rests

Tool rests are subject to heavy wear during everyday turning and will benefit from occasional dressing. It's surprising to realize one day that there is a definite low spot in the center of your metal rest, to say nothing of a multitude of nicks and dents. The best tool for removing these imperfections is a large, single-cut mill file in either bastard or first cut (a double-cut file will not work for this process). Draw-file the rest by turning the file sideways and alternately pulling and pushing it over the rest, much as if it were a spokeshave. You'll be rewarded with long ribbons of steel or iron.

Draw-filing also allows you to reshape a rest to your own needs. No two manufacturers make their rests quite the same, and the best edge shape is a matter of considerable debate. The illustration on the facing page shows my personal preference for a tool-rest shape. This design places the fulcrum point close to the work for good leverage and offers good support of the tool in all types of turning (unlike rests of flatter design).

Although the standard tool rest that comes with your lathe is adequate for most turning operations, it's worth making special tool rests to speed up production work. Tool rests are quite easy to fabricate from structural steel. Use a short length of cold rolled steel of the appropriate diameter for the neck, and braze or weld a piece of flat stock to it at the proper angle. Once the rest is welded, draw-file the top to the desired shape. If you don't have welding equipment, any welder can do the job for you at a nominal price. I've made 18-in.-long rests in this way, as well as odd-shaped rests for special situations. A handy shape is an S-curve: It allows you to turn the inside of a bowl from one end of the rest and the outside from the opposite end.

Smooth Running

Rewax your tool rest before every turning session to keep tools sliding smoothly.

Draw-filing is the best way to redress a misshapen tool rest.

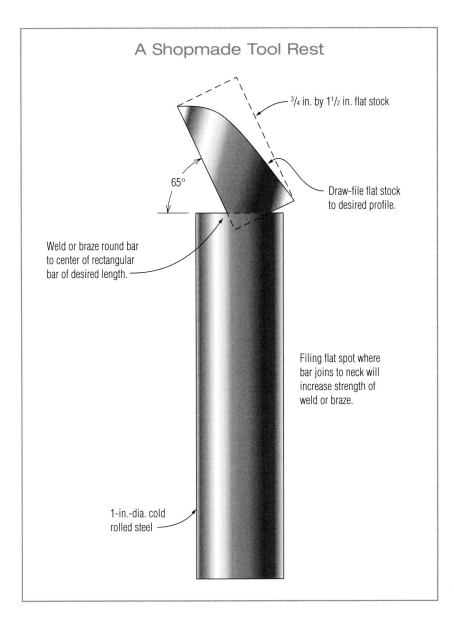

A Shopmade Tool Rest

¾ in. by 1½ in. flat stock

Draw-file flat stock
to desired profile.

65°

Weld or braze round bar
to center of rectangular
bar of desired length.

Filing flat spot where
bar joins to neck will
increase strength of
weld or braze.

1-in.-dia. cold
rolled steel

Modifying a Lathe

Now and again a job will come along that's just a bit beyond the capacity
of your lathe. For want of a couple inches of swing, you end up modifying
the entire project to make the one turning slightly smaller. One way to get
around this problem is to increase the swing of your lathe. As long as the
headstock is a separate piece (not cast as part of the bed), you can unbolt
it and interpose a couple of wood blocks to raise it up. You'll have to find
a longer bolt or bolts to hold it down, and there is a definite limit as to
how much you can raise things up—typically about 1 in. on smaller lathes
and up to 2 in. on larger machines. Swing is increased by double these
amounts. You may also have to find a longer belt. If you need to use the

tailstock, block it up in the same way. (A word of caution: Make sure you run your new blocked-up lathe at low speed.)

It's also possible to stretch a lathe so you can turn long work such as porch columns and canopy-bed posts. Bench lathes are quite easy to stretch. Simply bolt the bed to a plank of suitable length, then bolt the tailstock to a block at the end of the plank that raises it to the proper height. For floor-model lathes, bolt a suitable wood extension to the bed,

Freeing Rusted and Seized Nuts, Bolts, and Parts

When restoring machinery, you are often presented with a truly seized bolt, nut, or other part—usually due to corrosion. No amount of twisting, prying, or pounding will get the offending parts loose. The solution is to use a "fine wrench," more properly called an oxi-acetylene torch. The trick is to heat the part in once place, as described for removing seized faceplates on p. 159. A student of mine brought in a tool base from a classic Walker Turner lathe with the tool rest seized in the tool base, an excellent example for the following photo essay.

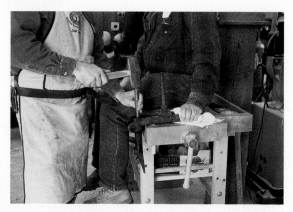

2 Once the assembly is dull cherry red, start working the parts free from one another. In the case of this tool rest, I placed a brass drift against it and pounded it out of the tool base. Be careful not to burn yourself.

1 Clamp the part in a vise and adjust the torch to a hot flame with a tip big enough to give plenty of heat. Heat one point on the periphery of the assembly (for nuts, heat one flat) until it is dull cherry red. (Reducing the room lights often helps to see this color change.) The flame should contact the work just above the inner blue cone, which is the hottest part of the flame. To prevent melting, always keep the torch moving, even if it is only an inch or so.

3 The freed parts.

TROUBLESHOOTING LATHE PROBLEMS

Problem	Cause	Solution
There is harmonic chatter in the work.	• The work is too thin for the length. • Bearings have failed or have insufficient preload.	• Cradle the work in your hand, use a heel cut with your skew, use a gouge, or employ a steady rest. • Adjust the preload or replace the bearings.
The knob or control is hard to turn.	• There are wood chips and dust in the thread. • The thread is stripped.	• Clean the threads. If necessary, run a tap into the internal thread and run a die over the external thread. • Replace parts; helicoil the internal thread (kits are available at auto parts stores).
The motor will not run.	• The motor is not plugged in. • A circuit breaker or fuse has blown. • The thermal switch in the motor has tripped. • A fuse has blown in the AC or DC variable-speed drive. • There is a brownout or no electricity. • The motor winding has burned out.	• Plug in the motor. • Reset the breaker or replace the fuse. • Reset the thermal switch (usually by pushing a button). • Replace the fuse. • Check with your electric company. • Rewind or replace the motor.
The tailstock and/or tool rest slides on the bed during turning operations.	• The bed has grease or finish on it. • The hold-down mechanism needs adjustment.	• Clean with the appropriate solvent. • Adjust the hold-down mechanism.
The tool does not move smoothly on the rest.	• The tool rest is dry. • The tool rest needs dressing.	• Wax the tool rest. • Dress and wax the tool rest.
Work slows down when you apply a tool.	• The tailstock is loose. • The belt is loose. • The key has come out of the motor or headstock pulley.	• Tighten the tailstock. • Tighten the belt. • Replace the key and tighten the grub screw, which locks it.
There is vibration.	• The work is out of balance. • A part is loose. • A belt is worn. • The motor or headstock pulleys are dirty or not concentric. • The pulleys are not in alignment. • The pulleys are out of balance. • There is a defective motor or a bent motor shaft. • The stand resonates.	• Round the work better with a band-saw and/or drawknife; change speed. • Find and tighten the loose part. • Replace the belt. • Clean or replace the pulleys. • Adjust the pulleys. • Have the pulleys balanced. • Repair or replace the motor. • Put sand bags in and/or on the stand.

or bolt the tailstock to a bench or table nearby. Remember that exact center alignment is of no great importance in spindle turning. With either setup, stretch a wooden tool rest from the tool base to the tailstock. You can also turn the piece by halves, turning it around in the lathe to do the second half. This way the standard tool rest is always over the bed of the lathe.

FINDING A MISSING PART for an otherwise great classic lathe can present a problem, since the manufacturer may have gone out of business long ago. The Internet has become a great resource for searching for parts. Also, want ads in woodworking magazines and club newsletters can yield results. The problem is you'll often have to buy an entire lathe to get the part you need.

Having the part made at a machine shop is often the best alternative, and prices can be quite reasonable—$100 to $200 for a part such as a spindle, pulley, or tailstock wheel. If you're considering buying a lathe that's missing major parts, such as a tailstock, check around before buying. Such a lathe is not worth much unless the manufacturer is still in business and parts are available.

Restoring a Used Lathe

Corrosion can be a chronic problem with lathes, and chances are that if you buy an old lathe it will have some rust (see photo essay on p. 162). To restore the machine to its former glory, you can use Klingspor's Sandflex blocks, emery paper, and steel wool. All are good weapons in the war on rust. For extremely heavy rusting with pitting, various proprietary preparations, often referred to as "naval jelly," work well. They loosen the surface rust and change the chemical nature of the rust in the pits, thereby preventing further rusting.

The buffers described on p. 89 are also useful for restoring metal parts. A spiral-sewn wheel with emery compound will make quick work of light rust on the exterior surfaces of small parts that can be carried to the buffer.

For the best finish for your used lathe, brush on one or more coats of machinery enamel, which is available at any hardware or paint store. It's best to remove any bolts and screws possible and to mask areas such as nameplates and bed ways with masking tape. Once the paint dries, remove the masking tape, replace the bolts and screws, and you have a classic restoration. To maintain your newly restored lathe (or any lathe) and prevent future rusting, get into the habit of wiping down the exterior surfaces with a rag on a regular basis, and always apply a thin film of paste wax to the bed after a turning session with green wood.

Turning Techniques

O nce you have your chucks and lathe tools (and you can sharpen them), it's time to do some turning—and have some fun. In this chapter, I will show you how to get through the basic tool moves without problems. I think gouges are the gateway to understanding tool use. If you can use a spindle gouge and a bowl gouge well, everything else will fall into place. It is like learning your first computer program. The rest are different but similar.

Coves and Beads

All spindle-turning shapes encompass the turning of either a cove or a bead, and mastering these two shapes will allow you to turn virtually any furniture spindle. Coves and beads are like compulsory figures in traditional ice skating—you can never practice them enough. Let's start with the cove, which can be cut only with a spindle gouge.

CUTTING A COVE

In its simplest form, a cove is a U cut down into the surface of a cylinder. The key to cutting any cove is to obey the Law of Perpendiculars; the illustration of a simple cove on p. 166, with perpendiculars constructed at four points, depicts this theory.

The idea is to start at the top edges of the cove and take a series of scooping cuts, always ending at the exact bottom. Start at the left edge of the cove with the gouge almost on its side and the flute pointing toward the center of the cove (see the illustration on the facing page). Bring the gouge to the center of the cove, rolling it to horizontal as the cut progresses. Next, repeat the motion from the right edge of the cove. Take a series of scooping cuts from each side until the cove is cut to the desired profile. Always cut downhill from the larger diameter to the smaller, and don't cut beyond the center of the cove bottom.

Rolling the gouge as the cut progresses is only part of the story. In addition to rolling, you must angle the tool left or right and slide it slightly forward to keep the bevel rubbing. A common mistake among beginners is to lock the handle of the gouge in one position against the hip and simply roll the tool in the prescribed manner. A catch is always the result, since the cove cut is not as simple as it seems. You're actually cutting a complicated compound shape, and if you simply roll the tool, you're not keeping the bevel rubbing. The illustration on the facing page shows the correct tool alignment. Pay particular attention to the handle and the large amount of left, right, and up-and-down movement required.

The most frequent mistakes when cutting a cove are failure to roll the gouge sufficiently (it should start almost on its side) and failure to angle the tool left or right sufficiently to have the bevel rubbing at the start of the cut. You must also slide the tool very slightly forward as the cut progresses because the diameter of the billet at the bottom of the cove is getting smaller, so the tangent point to the surface is moving away from the tool rest.

Another common mistake is using a gouge that is too wide for the cove. The cove must be wider than the gouge. Thus, it's useful to have a range of spindle gouges for cutting different-sized coves. I try to use a gouge that's about three-quarters the size of the cove I plan to cut.

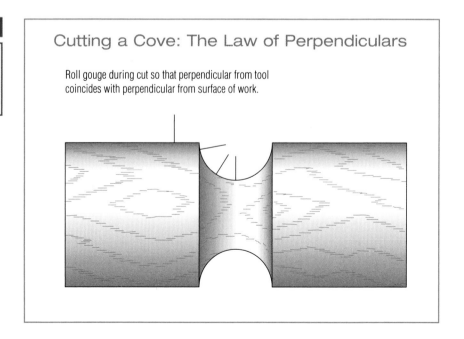

Cutting a Cove: The Law of Perpendiculars

Roll gouge during cut so that perpendicular from tool coincides with perpendicular from surface of work.

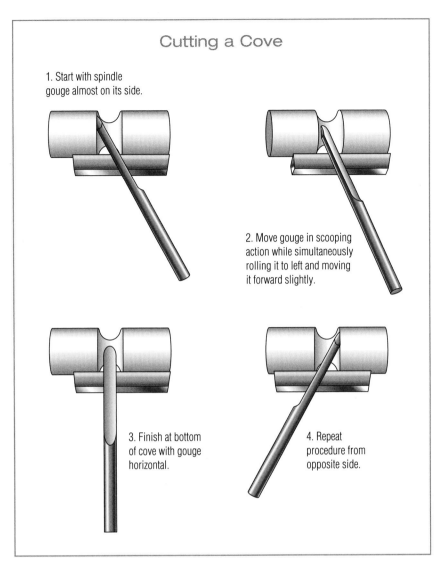

Cutting a Cove

1. Start with spindle gouge almost on its side.

2. Move gouge in scooping action while simultaneously rolling it to left and moving it forward slightly.

3. Finish at bottom of cove with gouge horizontal.

4. Repeat procedure from opposite side.

CUTTING A BEAD

The bead is the opposite of the cove, both in shape and in the way it is turned. It can be cut with either a gouge or a chisel (skew or beading-and-parting tool). Although it's exciting to cut beads with a skew a gouge is much better suited for beginners if not all turners. Cutting a bead with a spindle gouge is simple and straightforward, whereas using a chisel requires a precise sense of being flat on the bevel.

As a woodworker, I find that I do my turning in spurts when I need parts, and there are usually long lulls between sessions. After such a hiatus, it takes an hour or so of turning for my skills to return. During this acclimatization period, I'm hard-pressed to turn a bead with a skew and I frequently catch, though once I'm back in the groove again it's a simple matter. Therefore, the only beads I cut with a skew are during turning demonstrations to show others how to do it.

The Right Gouge

Beads are best turned with a spindle gouge. You will get much more consistent results (and much less ruined work) than with a skew.

When making furniture, whether professionally or for your own pleasure, time is money. You're dealing with expensive billets of wood that take time to prepare, and you can't afford to waste them. A catch with a chisel is a catastrophic event that generally relegates the work to the firewood pile. Even if this only happens once in every six or eight pieces, it's still a great waste. You'll save time and money by taking the time to reach for a gouge. Therefore, I strongly recommend that you use a gouge exclusively for cutting beads. Not only will you cut a cleaner bead of better profile, but also you'll have a better rate of success. Reserve the skew for planing cylinders and gentle tapers.

The first task in cutting a bead is laying it out. Experience will allow you to draw two pencil lines to mark the width of the bead, then proceed to cut it directly into the surface of a cylinder. At first, you're better off

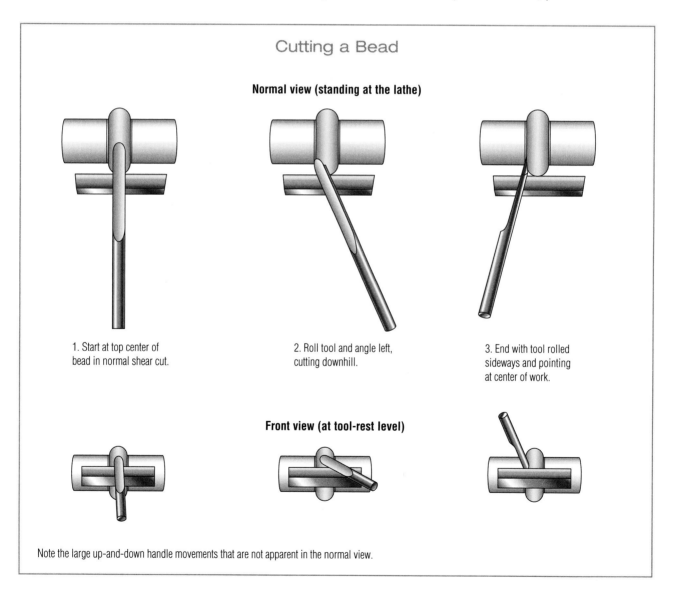

Cutting a Bead

Normal view (standing at the lathe)

1. Start at top center of bead in normal shear cut.

2. Roll tool and angle left, cutting downhill.

3. End with tool rolled sideways and pointing at center of work.

Front view (at tool-rest level)

Note the large up-and-down handle movements that are not apparent in the normal view.

Cutting a Bead with a Gouge

The beginner is well advised to start by cutting away either side of the spot where you are going to cut your bead to form a rondel. A rondel is no more than a raised ridge, but it will help you cut your first beads with plenty of clearance to the left and right.

1 Begin with the gouge flute up at the center of the rondel.

2 Angle the tool to one side and roll it downhill, sliding it back slightly on the tool rest.

3 Raise the tool handle and push forward as you approach the bottom of the bead. The handle has to be brought around to the right a bit as well to keep curvature to the bead. The cut ends with the gouge dead on its side with the very tip cutting. If you pushed farther, you would go through the exact center of the work.

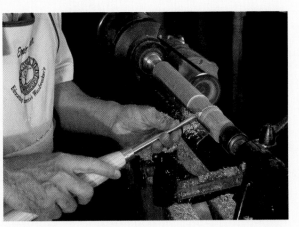

4 Return to the center of the bead and start cutting to the left. Repeat the procedure on the other side.

EVERYBODY, EVEN AN EXPERIENCED turner, makes a mistake at the lathe now and then. Although it's tempting just to throw the work in the corner and start again, there are a number of ways to sweep the blemish under the rug, so to speak. For example, you can widen or slightly deepen a cove and cut beads to a lower profile. You're probably the only one who will ever know about such subtle changes. If you break a piece off a bead, you can glue it back on (assuming, of course, that you can find it amongst the shavings under your lathe). If you can't find the chip, you can always plane the spot flat with a handplane, glue a new piece on, and re-turn the work. You can often turn a chipped corner or bead to the inside of the finished piece of furniture during assembly. Just think of it as "antiquing."

A handy glue to use for repairs is cyanoacrylate, or Super Glue. To fix a small blemish caused by a catch, fill the area with glue and sprinkle some shavings into the glue. On some woods, this can be a very convincing fix. Cyanoacrylate glue is also good for arresting checks at the end of a workpiece and for gluing small objects to a glue block.

Cyanoacrylate glue is available from woodworking suppliers and model shops in three viscosities: water thin, medium (my preferred grade), and thick. A catalyst is also sold that will speed up setting time to 20 to 30 seconds. Take care when working with this glue, since it will glue skin instantly. Avoid the temptation to hold the work with your fingers while the glue sets, or you may end up glued to the work. Cyanoacrylate glue is also very irritating to the eyes, so always wear safety glasses and work with plenty of ventilation.

For architectural turnings that are going to be painted, you can patch holes with auto-body putty (Bondo is a common brand). This material can even be used to replace broken beads: Patch the break with a blob of the putty, then re-turn.

Stick shellac works wonders for small blemishes. If you use a black stick shellac on cherry, it will look just like a pitch pocket. Remember there are no mistakes, just new design opportunities.

Handplaning Cylinders

If your skew skills are weak, you may use a handplane to clean up long cylinders and gentle tapers such as those found on Greek columns. I like to use an O5 Jack, resting the rear portion of the plane on the rest and centering the mouth over the work. A bit of fiddling is necessary until you produce a good curling chip; skewing the plane a bit to the work usually helps.

using the toe of a skew chisel to demarcate the limits of the bead. Although you can cut a bead directly into the surface of the cylinder, it's a good idea for beginners to cut away the area on either side to leave a raised square ridge, properly called a rondel. Raising a rondel first allows you to cut your bead without the worry of the bottom edge of the gouge catching on the adjoining surfaces. To raise the rondel, use the toe of a skew chisel as described for turning square to round with a shoulder, then use a parting tool to remove the adjacent material (see pp. 135–136).

Whether you're starting with a rondel or cutting directly into the surface of a cylinder, start in the middle of the bead in a classic shear cut, with the gouge held at 90° to the axis of the lathe and the flute facing up (see the illustration on p. 168 and the photo essay on p. 169). If you're cutting into the surface directly, you'll have to open up the areas adjacent to the bead slightly—either with your gouge or with the toe of a skew.

To cut the left side of the bead, angle the tool left, slide it back slightly on the tool rest, and roll it in the direction of the cut. Next, raise the handle until the tool is on its side and aimed at the center of the work (the tool is now aligned with a radius of the work). Push forward until you reach the bottom of the bead. As the cut progresses, you'll also have to swing the handle around behind the tool to create the curve of the bead and keep the bevel rubbing.

Most beginners fail to lift the handle high enough or roll the tool exactly on its side at the final stage of the cut. With the tool rolled only 45° and the handle raised only slightly, the result is invariably a catch on the adjoining surfaces. Another common mistake is failing to swing the handle around behind the cut but rather simply to push the gouge forward to the bottom of the bead, which results in a 45° flank instead of a rounded form.

To cut the right side of the bead, return to the center and reverse the procedure. Most beginners have difficulty making both halves of a bead symmetrical, but this comes with practice. The nice thing about using a gouge is that you can easily fine-tune a lopsided bead by recutting it by halves. Although you can do the same thing with a skew, it's much more difficult to produce a bead with a flowing profile.

One final note about beads. Most people today think of a bead as simply an oval ridge on the surface of a cylinder. In former times, however, turners always took the toe of a skew and incised a small groove, or bevel, at each edge of the bead where it meets the cylinder. On most furniture turnings, this grooving entails only a light scribing cut with the toe of a skew, while on larger architectural turnings, a definite groove is incised with repeated cuts of the skew.

Beveling the bead is a basic technique that adds tremendous visual impact to any turning by giving depth to the bead and setting it off from the surrounding spindle. On architectural turning, the bevel gives paint a place to flow, preventing a buildup of paint at the transition point and a loss of visual impact. One reason that machine turnings look so lifeless is that they're made on cutterhead lathes that cannot cut bevels or undercuts. As a hand turner, you have a real advantage in creating shapes that can grab the eye of the viewer.

Turning Square to Round

One of the most frequent questions I'm asked in spindle-turning classes is, "How do I get from square to round without breaking out the corners?" The answer I always give is to use sharp tools and shear-cutting techniques. The actual mechanics of the cut depend on whether you want the transition from square to round to be a square shoulder or a concave or convex radius. Let's start with the square shoulder.

Matching Beads

To cut small beads that match exactly, nothing beats a form scraper. Simply grind the profile you desire into the end of a scraper, and make as many exactly matching beads as you want.

The best way to cut a square shoulder is to use the toe of a skew chisel. You must hold the tool with the long corner down, its edge on the rest, and the bevel at 90° to the work (see the illustration below). This entails swinging the handle about 21°, which is half of the 42° inclusive grind angle. Use as much speed as is safe for the situation—1,100 rpm to 1,700 rpm for standard furniture turnings.

Start by lightly scoring the work, then move to the right (for a shoulder on the left) and widen the score mark. Go back and score the original mark deeper, then move to the right and remove the waste. This process is much like chopping a tree—the cut must always be wider than the inclusive grind angle of the chisel. Do this until the work is scored all the way around, and you are left with a square shoulder on the left and a sloping cut on the right that meets up with the shoulder. Finally, use a spindle gouge to trim away the excess material up to the shoulder.

For this process to work, the tool should be level on the rest and touching at the exact centerline of the work; only the very toe should touch. The tool's cutting edge must be absolutely vertical because slanting it one way or the other will cause it to walk in that direction. Some care is necessary to use the tool with a light touch and to read the ghost so that the tool returns to the previous cut each time.

Often the transition from square to round is a concave or convex radius. Cutting the radius entails carefully reading the ghost, bringing a spindle gouge into a shear cut, and rolling either a cove or a bead, depending on the shape desired. Again, running the lathe between 1,100 rpm and 1,700 rpm will help. Read the ghost, then bring the heel of the bevel in contact with the corners of the work. This is a highly interrupted cut, and a light but firm touch works best. Trying to force the cut without the bevel rubbing will result in a catch and likely broken corners. Multiple passes are necessary, and restarting requires careful reading of the ghost.

Faceplate Turning

The majority of faceplate work is done with a bowl gouge. Due to the grain orientation, you cannot use a spindle gouge (at least in the way you have in cutting beads and coves) because it will cause a nasty catch. A bowl gouge solves the problem nicely.

A bowl gouge cuts parallel to the axes of rotation. You should place the tool level to very slightly uphill on the rest (see the illustration on the facing page). The tool rest should be slightly below center so that the tip of the nose bevel touches the center of the work when the gouge is level on the rest. Your right hand controls 90% of the bowl gouge's movement, while your left hand mostly acts as a sand bag to hold the tool down on the rest. Twisting the tool with the right hand controls the quality of the cut, while swinging the tool to the left or right controls the direction of cut. Pushing forward on the handle (along its axes) controls the speed of the cut.

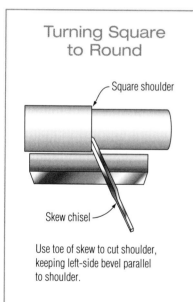

Turning Square to Round

Square shoulder

Skew chisel

Use toe of skew to cut shoulder, keeping left-side bevel parallel to shoulder.

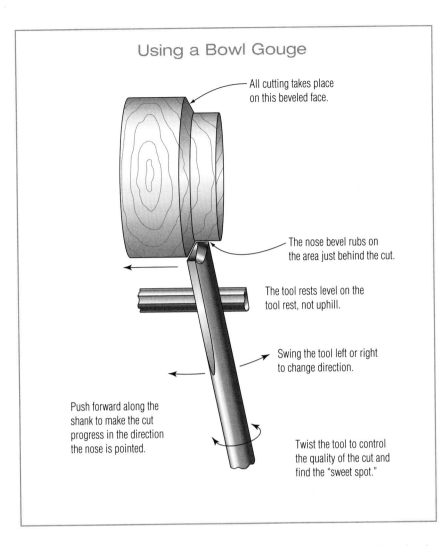

Using a Bowl Gouge

All cutting takes place on this beveled face.

The nose bevel rubs on the area just behind the cut.

The tool rests level on the tool rest, not uphill.

Swing the tool left or right to change direction.

Push forward along the shank to make the cut progress in the direction the nose is pointed.

Twist the tool to control the quality of the cut and find the "sweet spot."

Starting the tool can be tricky and requires aiming the nose bevel in the direction you want to cut. Depending on the angle of the nose bevel, the handle may be at what seems an odd angle. Hold the tool firmly down on the tool rest with your left hand, and lightly touch the work with the bottom half of the tool (see the the top photo on p. 174).

Once the cut is underway, you want to look for the "sweet spot," the position where the tool cuts the best. You can find this spot by twisting the tool ever so slightly to the left or right (see the bottom photo on p. 174). You are looking for the point where the bottom bevel rides on the ledge that has been created ahead of the cut. This leaves the nose bevel riding on the area just behind the cut, which serves to guide the tool. With a little practice, finding the sweet spot becomes a natural, involuntary action.

You direct the tool by swinging the handle to the left or right. The nose bevel is riding on the area just behind the ledge created by the cut, and the bottom half of the bevel is cutting away on the face of this ledge.

Bowl Gouges

Since most of the control of a bowl gouge is in your right hand, your left is only a weight to keep the tool from bouncing on the rest. When learning to use this tool, a good test is to remove your left hand periodically (or only use your index finger to hold it down) and see if it continues to cut in the same manner. If everything is right, you should be able to cut with just your right hand.

Start the cut by aiming the nose bevel in the direction you want to cut and touching the bottom half of the flute to the work.

Once the tool starts cutting, twist the tool slightly right or left until you find the "sweet spot."

The point of the nose-bevel contact becomes a fulcrum point as you swing the handle left or right and makes for a smooth transition in direction. You should keep the tool fairly flat on the rest during the entire operation. Do not use your left hand to pull or push the tool; push forward with your right hand along the tool's axis to make the tool go forward. After the tool is started, if everything is cutting correctly, you should be able to do the entire operation with your right hand and drop your left next to your side.

Start an inside cut exactly as shown in the top photo on the facing page. Here I have found the sweet spot, and the cut is proceeding normally. Push forward on the tool to advance it.

As you approach the center of an inside cut, the diameter is decreasing so the tool needs to be rotated to keep the cut sweet.

At the center, the flute should point almost straight up.

Sanding

While one of the main purposes of this book is to teach methods that eliminate excessive sanding, there comes a point in most turnings where some sanding is necessary. If you use the shear-cutting methods I've recommended, you should be able to start sanding for spindle turning at 150 grit or 180 grit rather than 60 grit or 80 grit, which would be the case if you were scrape-cutting. Sanding facework (in most woods) starts at a heavier grit—typically 60 grit or 80 grit.

SANDING SPINDLE WORK

When sanding spindle work, the piece remains in the lathe. For beginners, it makes sense to remove the tool rest, but experienced turners work around the rest by sanding at the back of the piece. Never use a whole (or even a large) sheet of sandpaper because it can wrap around the spindle and drag your fingers in with dire results. I always tear sandpaper into quarter sheets, then fold these in half.

For spindle turnings, I generally start with 180 grit and finish with 220 grit, although you can go as fine as you like. The main thing is not to skip grades of sandpaper or you'll get scratch marks on the work. By using good spindle techniques, sanding is merely a final operation to remove fuzz and make things uniform in texture for finish. Once you've finished sanding, its a good idea to burnish a turning with a handful of chips to improve surface finish.

SANDING FACEWORK

Facework requires a good deal of sanding even when using textbook turning techniques. An experienced turner will spend as much time sanding facework as turning it. Start with 60-grit or 80-grit sandpaper to remove the tearout in the end grain, then work up through grades to the desired finish. A common sanding schedule might run 60, 100, 150, 220, and so on. If providence allows you to start at 80 grit, then the schedule might run 120, 180, 220.

Although hand-sanding works fine for spindle work, the best way to sand facework is with a flexible pad mounted in an electric drill (see the photo on p. 178). The rubber pad is flexible enough for most facework. There are various proprietary systems available, one of which uses hook-and-loop fasteners to attach the sanding media to the disk. Another system uses sanding circles that are backed with pressure-sensitive adhesive. A third system has a metal or plastic clutch glued to the back of the sanding circle. All three systems allow quick changing of abrasive to work up through finer grades. With the hook-and-loop and clutch systems, coarser grades can be reused if they're not expended.

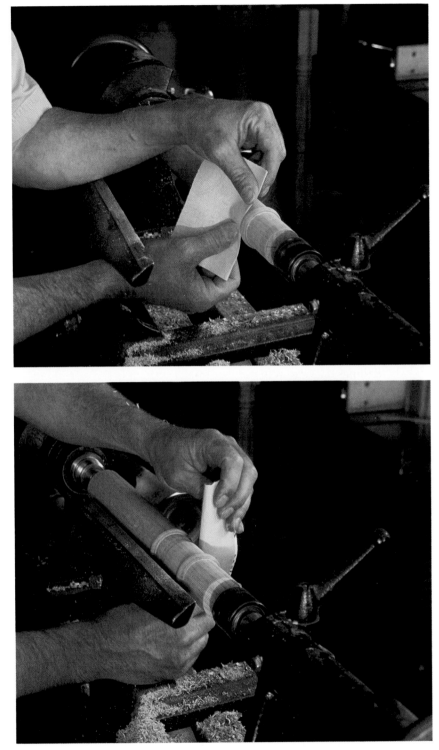

Beginners should slide the rest back out of the way during sanding (top), but experienced turners can sand opposite the rest so they don't have to remove it (bottom).

The easiest way to sand facework is with a sanding arbor mounted in an electric drill. Here I am using a shop-built hook-and-loop arbor that has sufficiently resilient padding to sand with the finest of grits without scratching.

Holding the spinning disk against the spinning work makes sanding go much faster than if you were sanding by hand. Since the disk wipes at an angle to the direction that the piece was turned, it produces a smoother surface. The important thing to remember when power-sanding is to spend enough time at the coarser grits to remove all of the tearout.

All of the clutch and some of the pressure-sensitive adhesive sanding systems are unsuitable for sanding beyond 180 grit because at finer grits there will be circular scratches even though the surface becomes more polished generally. The reason is that dirt and oversize sanding particles occasionally counteract the action of the majority of the sanding particles in the paper.

The solution is to glue foam rubber (I use ⅜-in. neoprene rubber) to an expended pad, then glue thin, flexible sandpaper to the foam. The resilience of the foam combined with the flexibility of the thin paper allows you to sand ultra-fine grades with ease. A thin piece of garnet or aluminum-oxide sandpaper glued to the foam rubber with photo-mount adhesive works splendidly. When the sandpaper needs changing, some heat from a hair dryer will loosen the glue joint so you can remove the sandpaper.

French Polishing

This is my favorite lathe finish. It is quick to apply and dries instantly—just the finish to use on Christmas Eve.

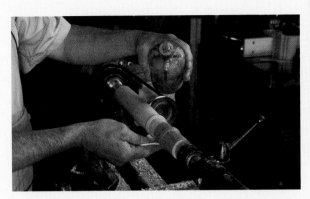

1 To French-polish in the lathe, apply a coat of the shellac mixture to the work with a small rag or a full brush. However you apply the shellac, be sure to saturate the work completely—don't worry if some of it dribbles onto the lathe bed. Brushes may be cleaned completely and inexpensively with a mixture of ammonia and water.

2 Remove the tool rest, stand aside, and start the lathe. You need plenty of speed—at least 1,700 rpm. Grab a handful of shavings and apply them with firm pressure to the spinning work. Turn the shavings often since they will become saturated with the excess shellac. The shellac will melt under the burnishing action of the shavings, leaving a pleasing French polish with none of the fuss, pumice, oil, and other assorted trappings of conventional French polishing.

3 French polish is a very thin finish, yet it is quite durable, except to prolonged contact with water, which will leave a white mark. To give the finish some water-resistance and further beauty, I apply pure carnauba wax to the spinning work. Pure carnauba, which is difficult to find, is very hard and shatters like ice if dropped. Crayon the wax onto the work (left) and finish by burnishing with shavings again (right).

4 The finished piece.

Finishing

Just as the lathe can be a great aid in reducing the drudgery of sanding, it can also help in the finishing process. In most cases, turned furniture parts will be finished with whatever is planned for the rest of the piece, and a considerable amount of time can be saved by finishing them right after they've been turned rather than when the piece is assembled. As outlined in chapter 4, it's a good idea to reference the turned piece to the drive center with a mark. This mark allows you to rechuck the piece with each of the center tines in the same place and maintain centering. For example, if you wanted 12 spindles, you would turn them all first, then rechuck and stain, and finally resand and finish.

Using a small rag, you can wipe on stains and most finishes while the lathe is running at a low speed. I use a rag about 2 in. square, which is small enough so that it won't pull your fingers in with it should it get caught in the spinning work—an important safety consideration. I often burnish an oil finish with shavings, usually about five minutes after applying the finish. Since burnishing with shavings wipes across the grain, there is good filling of pores.

One finish that's easy to apply with the workpiece in the lathe merits special mention. This is a lathe-applied French polish, which gives all the beauty of the traditional method but takes much less time and bother. To French-polish turner-style, you need to use genuine orange shellac made from shellac flakes. The canned variety has preservatives and extenders to prolong shelf life, which render it unsuitable for French polish.

I mix my shellac in 200ml plastic camping bottles, filling each bottle about one-quarter full of shellac flakes and adding alcohol to just shy of the top. I shake the bottle well and shake again every hour or so until everything dissolves, then set it in direct sunlight for at least a day. The wax and impurities settle out. I decant the liquid, which is pure orange shellac, and throw away the sediment.

Glossary

Bead A raised, convex ridge on the surface of a turning.

Beading-and-parting tool A very small double-bevel chisel that can be used for turning beads. It's also useful for sizing tenons and, in combination with calipers, for sizing work. The inclusive grind angle between the two bevels is typically about 42°.

Bed The rail-like platform on which the headstock, tailstock, and tool base mount. The two strips that form the rails are called ways and are made of wood, cast iron, or structural steel. The tailstock and tool base can easily slide back and forth on the ways but can be locked fast as necessary.

Bedan A single-bevel chisel that is used much the same as the beading-and-parting tool. The bevel is ground to about 30°.

Bevel The ground face of a turning tool that forms the cutting edge. Also a small cut at each edge of a bead, usually done with a skew.

Bowl gouge A gouge for faceplate work. It has an asymmetrical flute, and the bevel is ground to a variety of forms depending on the turning situation.

Bowl lathe A very short bed lathe, often without a tailstock, that is used exclusively for faceplate work. Its name derives from its popularity with bowl turners.

Catch The nick that occurs when the tool edge digs into the work after control is lost.

Centerline A line along the edge of the work at the same height as the centers (not to be confused with the true centerline, which lies along the longitudinal axis of the workpiece). This would be at 9 o'clock when viewing the work from the tailstock end.

Chatter work Decorative patterns created in the end grain by a small scraping tool of thin section, presented in such a way that it vibrates at a given frequency to create the pattern. *See also* Harmonic chatter.

Clearance angle The angle between the bevel of a tool and the surface of the work.

Collet chuck A metal chuck with a slotted cylinder that can be tightened around the work or expanded inside the work.

Cone chuck *See* Tapered mandrel.

Cove A U-shaped depression cut into the surface of a workpiece. It is the opposite shape to the bead.

Cup center A device with a center point on a Morse-taper shank of the appropriate size with a raised ridge around it (also called a ring center). It allows the tailstock to hold the work both radially and axially.

Cup chuck *See* Jam chuck.

Cutoff tool *See* Parting tool.

Dead center A cup or 60° center that mounts in the tailstock spindle to hold work. It does not spin with the work, hence its name. It both holds the work radially and acts as the bearing on which the work rotates.

Dressing The act of refacing a grinding wheel to make it round and bring fresh, sharp grinding particles to the surface. This is done with a diamond- or star-wheel dresser.

Drill chuck *See* Jacobs chuck.

Drive/spur center A center on a Morse-taper shank of the appropriate size with a central point surrounded by two or four sharp tines that engage the work. On lathes with a solid spindle, the drive center sometimes screws on the spindle.

Duplicator A mechanical device that mounts on a lathe and allows you to copy any turned workpiece.

Faceplate A cast-iron, steel, or aluminum-alloy disk that can be threaded onto the headstock spindle. There are one or more circles of holes around the periphery for screws to hold work to the surface of the plate.

Faceplate turning Any turning situation in which the grain of the work is at right angles to the axis of the lathe bed.

Flute A cove that runs the length of a spindle turning rather than around it. Also the concave groove along the shaft of a turning tool.

Form tool A scraper ground to a specific form. It allows convenient duplication of the shape and in some instances will make cuts that are not possible with any other tool.

Gap A dip in the bed just in front of the headstock on some lathes. It allows faceplate work of greater swing to be mounted in this area.

Ghost The hard-to-distinguish pattern created by the corners of the work spinning in the lathe before it is round. Seeing the ghost is an important part of turning from square to round.

Glue block A disk of wood slightly larger than the faceplate that is glued to the work for chucking.

Grind angle The inclusive angle from the back of a tool to the bevel.

Harmonic chatter A spiral pattern in spindle work caused when the work becomes thin enough to vibrate.

Headstock The heart of the lathe. It contains the spindle and assorted bearings. Pulleys on the spindle are belted to the motor. The spindle nose is threaded for faceplates and typically has a Morse-taper socket.

High Wycombe lathe A wood-bed lathe peculiar to the High Wycombe area of England. It was popular with the bodgers who turned furniture parts in the forests in that area. Today, any wood-bed lathe is referred to as a High Wycombe lathe.

Hollow grind The hollowing of a tool bevel produced by the convex surface of the grinding wheel.

Index head A mechanism that locks the headstock spindle at regularly spaced intervals so that layout or auxiliary operations with a router can be performed.

Interrupted cut A cut made on work that is not perfectly round. The tool is cutting the work some of the time and cutting air the rest. Needless to say, the tool is much more difficult to control in an interrupted cut.

Jacobs chuck A key-type three-jaw chuck for holding drills in the headstock or tailstock.

Jam chuck A wooden chuck, made on a faceplate, that resembles a cup. The work is held in a tapered pocket scraped into the interior of the cup.

Laying grain down Cutting downhill on the grain.

Live center A tailstock center, either cup or 60°, that has bearings so that it can turn with the work.

Long-corner chisel *See* Skew chisel.

Morse taper A system of tapers (about 3° inclusive) that allows accessories to be mounted in the headstock or tailstock spindle.

Offset turning A turning situation where the workpiece is offset from the original starting center at one or both ends. (The crankshaft of a car is turned in this way.)

Outboard turning A situation where faceplate work is not turned over the bed of the lathe. On some lathes, the headstock swivels so that the work spins in front of the bed. On others, the back end of the headstock spindle is left-hand threaded to receive a special faceplate.

Paper joint A glue joint in which kraft paper is interposed in the glueline. This allows a spindle turning to be divided lengthwise into two, four, or more pieces. It also can be used for faceplate turnings and as a chucking method to attach a glue block to the work.

Parting The act of severing the work from the lathe with a parting tool to cut a spindle turning at an appropriate point or to cut facework from the faceplate.

Parting tool A tool for parting work from the lathe.

Pattern stick A thin strip of wood on which a full-scale drawing of the piece to be turned is laid out. Notches at appropriate points allow the information on the pattern stick to be transferred to the work with a pencil.

Planing cut The cut made by a skew chisel when it's cutting properly (so called because the geometry of the cut is similar to that made by a handplane).

Pressure turning A chucking method in which the work is held on a glue block by the pressure of the tailstock spindle acting through a live center. It allows quick chucking and unchucking and leaves no marks on the work.

Rake angle The angular distance from the top surface of the tool, just behind the cutting edge, to the surface of the work.

Reed A bead that runs the length of a spindle turning rather than around it.

Rondel A raised square ridge running around a spindle turning.

Roughing out The act of bringing a square turning billet round.

Roughing-out gouge A large, U-shaped gouge for roughing out.

Scrape cut The term has two meanings. One is when a normal turning tool is used incorrectly without the bevel rubbing. This entails presenting the tool at right angles to the work on the centerline rather than in a shear cut—a situation to be avoided. The second meaning is when a tool is intentionally sharpened to a burr and presented downhill. This is actually a shear cut because the burr is cutting at a highly positive angle.

Scraper Any tool ground or burnished to a burr and presented downhill.

Screw chuck A chuck consisting of a simple wood screw onto which the workpiece is threaded.

Scroll chuck A metal chuck with three or four jaws that open or close in unison through the action of a scroll controlled by a key or levers.

Shear cut A cut made when the bevel of a turning tool is presented tangentially to the surface of the work. This gives a positive-rake-angle cut that pares wood and leaves a good surface finish.

Skew chisel A double-bevel chisel with the edge skewed 15° to 20° from 90° and an inclusive angle of grind of 42° or less.

Spindle This term has two meanings. First, it can refer to any spindle-turned workpiece. Second, it refers to the shaft in either the headstock or tailstock. The headstock spindle is set in bearings and has a nose thread to accept faceplates. The tailstock spindle is often referred to as the ram. Both spindles typically have Morse-taper sockets to accept accessories.

Spindle gouge A gouge with a flute of constant radius and ground to a fingernail point. It is the basic tool of any spindle turner because it handles most spindle-turning situations.

Spindle turning Any turning situation in which the grain of the workpiece runs parallel to the bed of the lathe.

Steady rest A device that supports a spindle turning at some point near its center and dampens vibration, hence eliminating harmonic chatter.

Story stick A thin strip of wood with notches cut at key points used in the layout of a spindle turning. It is a great aid in duplication.

Swing The capacity of a lathe, which is twice the height of the center above the bed. The true capacity of any lathe, however, is the swing above the tool base.

Tailstock A metal casting containing a spindle, or ram, that opposes the headstock. Its function is to hold pressure through a center on spindle work and to hold accessories such as drills while they act on work mounted on the headstock.

Tapered mandrel A chuck that is a tapered (about 3°) rod. Hollow work can be held on a tapered mandrel for turning the outside of the piece.

Tearout A surface imperfection produced when the grain is torn from the surface of the wood rather than pared away. This is most often a problem in the end grain of facework and requires heavy sanding to remove.

Tool base A metal casting that attaches to the bed and holds the tool rest. It should lock solidly on the bed yet be able to be moved quickly and easily to any location or angle.

Tool rest A T-shaped casting that mounts in the tool base and supports turning tools while they act on the workpiece.

Torus A doughnut-shaped surface generated by a circle rotated about an axis in its plane that does not intersect the circle.

Way One of the two rails that form the lathe bed.

Resources

The following companies sell lathes, turning tools, various accessories, finishes, and safety equipment, either through distributors or mail order. Many offer a catalog; call or write for the cost and other information. This list also includes publishers of woodturning magazines and companies and individuals who offer woodturning classes.

Airware America
Highway 54 South
P. O. Box 975
Elbow Lake, MN 56531
(218) 685-4458
(800) 328-1792
Air helmets and other safety equipment

American Association of Woodturners
667 Harriet Ave.
Shoreview, MN 55126
(612) 484-9094
American Woodturner magazine

Arrowmont School of Arts and Crafts
Box 567
Gatlinburg, TN 37738
(615) 436-5860
Turning classes

Brookfield Craft Center
286 Whisconier Rd.
P. O. Box 122
Brookfield, CT 06804
(203) 775-4526
Turning classes

Conover Workshops
18125 Madison Rd.
P. O. Box 679
Parkman, OH 44080
(440) 548-3491
Turning classes

Constantine
2050 Eastchester Rd.
Bronx, NY 10461
(800) 223-8087
Lathes, turning tools, accessories, finishes (including shellac flakes)

Craft Supplies USA
1287 E. 1120 St.
Provo, UT 84601
(800) 551-8876
(801) 373-0917
Lathes, turning tools, accessories, turning classes

Delta International Machinery Corp.
4825 Highway 45
North Jackson, TN 38305
(901) 363-8800
Lathes

Eagle America
124 Parker Ct.
P. O. Box 1099
Chardon, OH 44024
(800) 872-2511
(216) 286-9334
Lathes, accessories, special router bits for lathe work

David Ellsworth
Fox Creek
1378 Cobbler Rd.
Quakertown, PA 18951
(215) 536-5298
Turning classes

Garrett Wade Company
161 Ave. of the Americas
New York, NY 10013
(212) 807-1155
Lathes, turning tools, accessories

General Manufacturing Co.
835 Cherrier St.
Drummondville, Quebec J2B 5A8
Canada
(819) 472-1161
Lathes

Glaser Engineering Co.
P. O. Box 95
El Segundo, CA 90245-0095
(310) 823-7128
Turning tools, screw chucks

Grizzly Imports
P. O. Box 2069
Bellingham, WA 98227
(800) 541-5537
Lathes, turning tools

Guild of Master Craftsmen
Castle Place
166 High St.
Lewes, East Sussex BN7 1XU
England
(01273) 477374
Woodturning magazine

Highland Hardware
1045 N. Highland Ave., NE
Atlanta, GA 30306
(800) 241-6748
(404) 872-4466
Lathes, turning tools, accessories,
turning classes

Lawler Gear Corp.
10220 E. 65th St.
Raytown, MO 64113
(800) 364-3038
Ornamental turning machines

Lee Valley Tools
1080 Morrison Dr.
Ottawa, Ontario K2H 8K7
Canada
(613) 596-0350
Lathes, turning tools, accessories

Oneway Manufacturing
241 Monteith Ave.
Stratford, Ontario N5A 2P6
Canada
(800) 565-7288
(519) 271-8441
Lathes, chucks, grinder rests,
diamond dressers

Packard Woodworks
101 Miller Rd.
P. O. Box 718
Tryon, NC 28782
(704) 859-6762
Lathes, turning tools, accessories

Robert Sorby Ltd.
Athol Rd./Woodseats Rd.
Sheffield S8 0PA
England
(0742) 554231
Turning tools

Rockler Companies Inc.
4365 Willow Drive
Medina, MN 55340
(800) 279-4441
Turning tools, specialty finishes

Surplus Center
P. O. Box 82209
Lincoln, NE 68501
(800) 488-3407
Vacuum pumps (new and used)

Trend-Lines Inc.
135 American Legion Hwy.
Revere, MA 02151
(800) 767-9999
Lathes, turning tools,
woodworking supplies

Woodcraft Supply Corp.
210 Wood County Industrial Park
P. O. Box 1686
Parkersburg, WV 26102-1686
(800) 225-1153
Lathes, turning tools, accessories

Woodworker's Supply
5604 Alameda Pl., NE
Albuquerque, NM 87113-2100
(800) 645-9292
Lathes, turning tools,
safety supplies, finishes

Index